Heath Lambert knows what it's like to experience God's love in the midst of great adversity. In this book, he pulls back the veil so we can see, in fresh and encouraging ways, God's boundless love and delight in his children.

—RANDY ALCORN, author of *Heaven*, *If God Is Good*, and *Deception*

This is a gloriously beautiful book, unlike anything I have ever read. As I write these words, I am a bit breathless and in awe. I am filled with gratitude and conviction by what I have seen of the love of God. Through the journey and words of Heath Lambert, I have luxuriated in the love of God like I never have before. Written out of the deepest and darkest days of physical and relational suffering, Heath takes you to the only place of true comfort in this sin-broken world, the eternally and gloriously beautiful love of God. I have never read such a thorough, tender, and compelling exposition of God's love in all my years of ministry. I am sad that decades ago I did not have the vision of this book in my heart. Get this book, spend time in it, not just once, but again and again, and watch what God will do in you and through you.

—PAUL DAVID TRIPP, bestselling author and the president of Paul Tripp Ministries

As Christians we know that God loves us. But when we, as Christians, endure times of sorrow and loss, times of poverty and want, times of illness and weakness, it is then that we need to *know* that God loves us. And as Heath Lambert so capably shows in this book, God really and truly does. Lambert searches the Bible to show that God's love for us is fixed and unwavering, steady and unchanging, grounded in eternity past and guaranteed to endure through the endless ages to come. To know of that love and to be reassured in it, I suggest you read this book and feast on its many treasures.

—TIM CHALLIES, author of *Seasons of Sorrow*

I have known and respected Heath Lambert for many years. I have known him in his roles as preacher, teacher, theologian, and counselor. I have known him both before and after his struggles with major brain surgery and a difficult recovery. I know that before his recent struggles, Heath solidly believed in the love of God. But now, with passion driven by Scripture and channeled through the intense experience of his momentous struggle, Heath Lambert can tell us about the love of God in a whole new dimension. His theological and biblical reflections about God's love are a great gift to the church. He is generous in sharing about his experience and generous in sharing biblical truth.

—R. ALBERT MOHLER JR., president of The
Southern Baptist Theological Seminary

We all know that God so loved the world that he gave his Son to die. This book supplies the missing pieces, showing us how God's love extends practically to our lives today—even amid our trials and unanswered questions. It will increase your understanding, build your faith, and show you that God's love is greater than you or I ever dreamed. Read it, be blessed, and pass it along to others.

—ERWIN W. LUTZER, pastor emeritus at Moody Church, Chicago

Deeply personal, refreshingly transparent, intensely engaging, and biblically faithful, *The Great Love of God* gives Heath's raw personal testimony attesting to the steadfast, satisfying, and practical love of God toward his children. Heath's musings will strengthen weary hearts and calm troubled souls with the everlasting truth of God's great love.

—T. DALE JOHNSON JR., executive director of the
Association of Certified Biblical Counselors, director of
counseling programs and associate professor of biblical
counseling at Midwestern Baptist Theological Seminary

Heath Lambert has an incredible story to tell about the love of God. His experience as a son, father, pastor, and preacher creates a fascinating window into profound theological truth. This book is biblical, practical, emotional, and challenging. Every believer and every church could benefit from reading it.

—JIMMY SCROGGINS, author and pastor of Family Church

James wrote, "Blessed is the man who perseveres under trial." Heath Lambert embodies that challenge and writes from first-hand experience. Having endured four brain surgeries and countless painful betrayals from fellow believers, Heath has the credibility to write about God's love in the midst of suffering. He makes this bold claim, "Great love defines God's essence and will transform your existence." Readers will find Heath's personal testimony captivating and his biblical insight into God's love transforming.

—BOB RUSSELL, retired senior minister,
Southeast Christian Church, Louisville, KY

Everything Heath Lambert writes is worth reading, but nothing more so than *The Great Love of God*. In this rich, accessible book Lambert approaches this most welcome topic in a way that is faithful to Scripture, full of pastoral insight, and, most movingly, illustrated by his first-person account of God's sustaining love during his own seasons of crisis and challenge. Every Christian will benefit from reading *The Great Love of God*.

—JASON K. ALLEN, president of Midwestern Baptist
Theological Seminary and Spurgeon College

THE GREAT
LOVE
OF
GOD

THE GREAT
LOVE
OF
GOD

Encountering God's Heart
for a Hostile World

HEATH LAMBERT

ZONDERVAN
REFLECTIVE

ZONDERVAN REFLECTIVE

The Great Love of God
Copyright © 2023 by Heath Lambert

Requests for information should be addressed to:
Zondervan, *3900 Sparks Dr. SE, Grand Rapids, Michigan 49546*

Zondervan titles may be purchased in bulk for educational, business, fundraising, or sales promotional use. For information, please email SpecialMarkets@Zondervan.com.

ISBN 978-0-310-14220-1 (softcover)
ISBN 978-0-310-14227-0 (audio)
ISBN 978-0-310-14226-3 (ebook)

Cover design: Tammy Johnson
Cover art: © Lurii Kuznetsov / Getty Images
Interior design: Sara Colley

Printed in the United States of America

23 24 25 26 27 28 29 30 31 /TRM/ 12 11 10 9 8 7 6 5 4 3 2 1

To my precious daughter, Chloe.
Some daddies have an Angel, and some daddies have a Princess,
But your daddy has an Angel-Princess;
And God loves you more than I—
What great love that must be!

Contents

Foreword

Countless authors have written about the love of God. Many are poets, others are pastors, and probably most are theologians. Each could tell you their insights on the doctrine of God's love, but those who write about the *greatness* of that love are different. They are most often Christians who have suffered and suffered hard.

I should know. At one time my broken neck and quadriplegia made me wonder, *what's so great about the love of God?* But after decades of questioning and searching, I came to see that our call to suffer is actually an outflow of God's love toward us. To encourage us, he will write some light moments into the script of our lives using adventure, pleasure, or romance. But without fail, some scenes are going to break your heart, some of your favorite characters will die, and the movie may end earlier than you wish.

But the tender love of God tempers the many trials that come to each of us, allowing only those difficulties that accomplish his good plan, for he takes no joy in human agony. In God's wisdom and love, every trial in a Christian's life is ordained from eternity past, custom made for that believer's eternal good, even when it doesn't seem like it. Nothing happens by accident ... not even tragedy ... not even sins committed against us.

That's not why the love of God is considered great. The greatest love scene in the world happened when Christ hung and bled on the cross. It was God saying, "Look, see, this is how much I love you!" And he played out this extraordinary love scene while we snubbed him in cool, calloused indifference.

This is why I am so enthusiastic about the book you hold in your hands, for it delves deeply into that very love. True, there will be some who find it ironic that a work titled *The Great Love of God* should be authored by a man who has suffered enormous pain, deep disappointment, and heartbreaking rejection, yet it is these hardships that give this volume its depth and integrity—not to mention its believability.

Heath Lambert is the one who has suffered and suffered hard. I came to know Heath when he served as the executive director of the Association of Certified Biblical Counselors (ACBC), one of the largest biblical counseling organizations in the world. I was touched by his skillful handling of the Word of God in counseling people who were suffering through their worst afflictions. He handled each individual with compassion, encouraging them to follow the path of God's Word toward wholeness and healing.

Then the tables turned. Heath was suddenly the one falling into suffering's deep abyss. Almost overnight, the consummate counsellor became the humbled counselee. Yet our man was not about to insist that God cough up the "reasons why" in exchange for his trust. He did not demand to see the blueprint before he bent his will to the Lord. Instead, Heath Lambert trusted in the greatness of God's love for him and his family. And his suffering—that silent, dark companion—slowly revealed new and wondrous insights into the *great* love of the Almighty.

It's what this book is all about. So I gladly commend to you *The Great Love of God*, for Heath Lambert is someone who has benefited from his own advice concerning suffering. And he is all the better for it. You can trust what this sage counselor has to say about the matchless supremacy of the love of God and its healing, transforming power. Listen to the kind and gentle man who has suffered, and you, too, will be "convinced that neither death nor life, neither angels nor demons, neither the present nor the future, nor any powers, neither height nor depth, nor anything else in all creation, will be able to separate us from the love of God that is in Christ Jesus our Lord" (Romans 8:38–39 NIV).

Joni Eareckson Tada
Joni and Friends International Disability Center
Agoura, California

CHAPTER 1

A Journey to the Heart of God

But God, being rich in mercy, because of the
great love with which he loved us . . .
EPHESIANS 2:4

God loves you.

God's love is greater than the measureless galaxies in the vast expanse of creation. It stretches eternally beyond the distant sun and plunges forever past the depths of the deepest sea. It is broader than the sprawling sky but nearer than the air in your lungs. God's love is more tender than a loved one's caress and more powerful than a supernova's blast. It is infinitely more beautiful than the glorious colors encompassing the setting sun. God's love existed forever before you were born. It will endure for an eternity after you die.

This love is different and better than any love you have ever experienced in your life. The love of every other person for you is based on something about you. They love you because you are their son or daughter, their husband or wife. They love you because you're cute, pretty, smart, or funny. They may love you because of something you did or did not do.

This is not the way God loves. Everyone else loves you because of something true about you. God loves you because of something true about him. It is God's nature to love. Nothing you have ever done or ever could do will make God love you. He loves you because of who he is, not who you are. God's love flows from the fact that he is God. Love is who God is and what God does.

God's love will never waver. If God's love were based on who you are, then you could change it. You could do something to make it start or stop. When God loves you, because it's his nature to love, his love for you will last as long as he does. The significance of this love will stretch into ten thousand forevers. It will transform everything about you.

The great love of God is his commitment, based on who he is, to delight in you, to give you wonderful things, and to protect you from harm. This love is the most precious reality in your life. You may not know it, but God's love defines you. God's love for you is the one thing in this world that gives your life meaning. God does not love you because you matter. You matter because God loves you.

The great goal of your life is that the great love of God would transform you into a person of great love. Once you know about and believe in God's love, you will cherish that love. You will love God back. You will love the people he has made in a way you never thought possible. Your whole life before the grave and beyond it will be consumed in dazzling and majestic love. All of your life and eternity stands on whether you grasp the significance of the great love of God.

God loves you.

Let me tell you about a fresh encounter I had with the great love of God in an operating room one ominously glorious morning.

MY EXPERIENCE OF THE HEART OF GOD

That morning came at me, dark and scary, like the approach of a shadowy stranger in the night. I awoke and drove to the hospital in the quiet of the early hours. Joining a somber line of patients in the registration area, I began to fill out a pile of forms longer than the lines in which we stood. As I affixed my signature to terrifying legal disclosures, my heart was processing more concern than my hands were paperwork.

That was the morning's most pleasant task, and, once completed, I sat in the waiting room with my wife. She clutched my hand in both of hers as the last precious moments clicked by. We prayed together. We kissed one another. Then the nurse took me back.

The next hour was unpleasant.

Medical preparation for brain surgery includes no joys. You must endure the foul odor of the antiseptic sponge bath, the unpleasant preparation of the scalp, and the insertion into your body of needles the size of missile silos.

Eventually my surgeon entered with a swarm of white coats explaining the surgery again and confirming my understanding of what was about to happen. In a strange, disconcerting moment of confirmation, he asked me to identify the side of my skull to be opened. The location of the surgery authenticated, he marked the right side of my scalp with a surprisingly unsophisticated purple marker and disappeared into the hall. I followed on a stretcher a few moments later.

The journey down the hallways toward the operating room took longer and was far more significant than I anticipated. Overpowered by dread, I had no expectation that, once in that operating room, I would experience an event infinitely more wonderful than surgery.

That journey through those meandering hallways changed my life. It was the culmination of the three hardest years of suffering I have ever endured. In those three years, I saw more evil than I had in my entire life and experienced more heartache than I ever imagined I could. The painful ordeal of those years was far worse than any medical problem and was something no surgery could fix.

I experienced personal hatred drastically more painful than I will ever be able to explain. In the years leading up to surgery, a heart-wrenching series of relational breaks happened in my ministry. The very best ministers and the greatest ministries go through seasons of challenge and difficulty, and those three years before my surgery were one of those hard seasons for me.

In this season in the life of our church, several people experiencing pain and frustration began to respond to me and my family in ways that were intentionally personal and obviously sinful. We suffered constant attacks and false allegations both in person and online. People I loved and trusted turned their backs on me and sought to destroy my reputation. My wife was mistreated by people who had been close to her. My young children experienced cruelty from people who called themselves Christians.

I have never endured such appalling and persistent acts of hatred. Many nights my wife and I sat alone on the floor of our bedroom crying over horrible things that we had no power to stop.

While I was experiencing this hatred in my personal life, my body started to behave strangely. The trouble began with subtle twitches, which I ignored, focusing instead on other more pressing matters. But the twitches got worse, and my family and friends started to notice them. Before long the twitches turned into uncontrollable spasms. I sought medical attention, and after ruling out the scariest options, we discovered that the problem was caused by a cluster of blood vessels compressing one of the nerves in my brain that controls movement on the right side of my body.

At first, we tried to address the problem with medicine. I received injections in my face, head, and neck to stifle the nerve endings so they would not do what my brain was telling them to do. The injections didn't work. As the symptoms worsened, I was increasingly unable to keep my eyes open or to speak or chew without difficulty. Eventually, five different neurosurgeons told me I would need brain surgery to relieve the pressure on the nerve and completely solve the problem.

EMBRACED BY LOVE

So, there I was that morning in the hospital on my way to an operation on my brain. I have used power drills enough times in my life that the thought of one being applied to my skull disturbed me. To fill my mind with God's truth, I had memorized Jesus's teaching on anxiety in Matthew 6:25–34, and I was praying through those verses as I was wheeled into the operating room.

The room filled with bright light and bustled with a team of medical professionals operating state-of-the-art equipment. Just as my eyes adjusted to the sight of the lights and people, my mind suddenly recalled Matthew 6:26, "Look at the birds of the air: they neither sow nor reap nor gather into barns, and yet your heavenly Father feeds them. Are you not of more value than they?"

When I saw that room and remembered those words . . . something happened to me.

God himself wrapped me in a personal embrace of his love.

In Matthew 6, Jesus says that God loves and cares for the birds by giving them everything they need even when they do no work on their own. After Jesus gets us thinking about God's love and care for the birds, he switches his focus to people and asks, Don't you think you're worth more than the birds? Don't you know that God loves you more than any sparrow?

As I thought about those words explaining God's love and looked around that operating room demonstrating God's love, I began to *experience* God's love in my heart in a way I had not experienced before. It was one of the most wonderful and comforting experiences of my life. In that moment, though it looked like I was lying on an operating table preparing for surgery, something far more real and profound was happening. I was standing in the midst of God's very own heart, consumed and embraced by his infinite love.

This embrace of God's love helped me to see my experience in an entirely new way. Although I lived in a hateful world filled with hateful people while experiencing an increasingly debilitating physical condition, God was providing for me far beyond my daily need for food and clothing. God had placed me in a sophisticated room filled with millions of dollars in medical equipment and people who had thousands of combined hours in training and experience at one of the elite medical centers in the world.

I knew God loved me. That was all that mattered. Despite the hateful treatment I'd received from people I loved and despite hateful problems threatening my way of life, I knew God loved me. That experience of the great love of God changed me.

My apprehensions faded, and I began to think differently about the terrible things I'd been experiencing. I had been embraced by the love of God, and lying there on the operating table, I had an overwhelming desire to experience more of this love and to tell others about it.

The doctors began to send me into a deep sleep, but in my last few seconds of conscious thought, I made a commitment to do whatever I could to find out more about God's love and to share it with others so that as many people as possible could experience the same love that had embraced me that morning.

MORE THAN MY PERSONAL JOURNEY

That small taste of the great love of God showed me the great need we all have for a fresh embrace of perfect love. Every person needs to be wrapped in the loving embrace of God. Nothing is more obvious about our world today than the reality of how far our culture has slipped from the ideal of divine love. At this time in human history, our society has sunk into the depths of darkness, desperation, and despair. An avalanche of problems overwhelm us. Consider just a few of them.

We are *hateful*. A cancer of hatred spreads through our entire society, evident in everything from racism to road rage. Vicious attacks on social media and savage political debates divide us. Many suffer bullying at school and in the office while painful cultural divisions, broken friendships, strife in our churches, and the breakup of marriages reveal a deeper hatred flowing from our hearts into the cracks in our society.

Having lost the ability to coexist with kindness, we spend much of our time wading through a swamp of hate-filled people who hate others and are hated by them in return. This cruel reality of life today overwhelms us, exhausts us, and discourages many.

We are *lonely*. With more than seven billion of us on the planet, you would think it is impossible to be lonely, but most of us are. Social media outlets designed to keep us in constant contact with others have not eradicated our loneliness but intensified it. Open sexual relationships promise boundless love but instead diminish intimacy, leaving us feeling empty and isolated. Shallow relationships in our homes, neighborhoods, offices, and places of worship make us feel disconnected even in rooms full of people.

We are *hurting*. This generation has witnessed painful revelations of the widespread abuse of authority. We have seen shocking disclosures of corrupt leadership from conservatives on Capitol Hill, liberals in Hollywood, trusted religious leaders, and many others. No sector of society has been immune from wicked leaders who betray our confidence, undermine our trust, and overwhelm us with pain. When a trusted authority deceives us and corrupts our confidence, the damage is extreme. Many have decided that no leader is trustworthy.

We are *scared*. A global pandemic erased the confidence the most self-sufficient among us once had. In our fearful desperation we sought comfort in social distancing, masks, vaccines, antibodies, hydroxychloroquine, and even vast stockpiles of toilet paper. Yet at every turn we came up short. No matter what we do, the troubles persist and the fear remains. Everywhere we look we find signs of upheaval we can't understand or control: tumult in foreign affairs, turbulence in the domestic economy, and turmoil in our streets tear apart the fabric of society. Countless unknowns make us fearful of what awaits us in the future.

We are *confused.* For every person who wants to know God, we must honestly admit that we more often misunderstand him. We do not know God nearly as well as we thought we did. We do not know *who* he is. We do not understand *what* he is doing. We have not experienced the warmth of his love and compassion. This loss that has left us cold, isolated, and disoriented.

Hatred, animosity, and cruelty in our world has brought us to a state of emergency, and a powerful display of infinite love is our only hope. In a crowded world, we are trapped in solitary confinement, and the only rescue we can find from our loneliness is in the acceptance of the one person whose great love we most need but stubbornly reject. Our quest for the perfect human leader repeatedly fails, but a perfectly trustworthy Leader in heaven searches for us and wants to share his love—a love that never fails, never betrays, and never abuses. As we squint in the darkness of chaos and anxiety, our only hope is to see the light of the One whose infinite love alone casts out fear. Now more than ever and more than anything, people must understand the character of the God whose great love makes us better, stronger, and wiser.

You need to be embraced by God's great love.

COME WITH ME TO THE HEART OF GOD

As I awoke from surgery and began the slow road of recovery, I immersed myself in the great love of God. I read the entire Bible from Genesis to Revelation and paid careful attention to all the passages that addressed the love of God. After that, I began to read all the books I could find about the love of God.

Many of these books were deeply moving and caused me to grow in appreciation of the divine love that had changed me and was continuing to change me. This time of reading and exploration continued the transformation God had begun in my life. Though I have spent several decades studying Scripture and have earned advanced degrees in theology, I had never before seen so clearly how the authors of the Bible talk about the love of God in ways that stir the soul and lift the heart to the heavens. Their vision of God increased my own appreciation of his love and has convinced me that I must tell others about it.

God loves you and longs to embrace you in his love. The more you and I are caught up into the great love of God, the more it will change our lives and revolutionize our world. There is power in the great love of God. There is power to change our hateful world into a world full of love and mutual care. There is power in the love of God to lift you out of the rut of loneliness that has had you trapped for so long. There is power in the love of God to transform your hard, selfish, and hateful heart into a soft heart that cares for others. There is power in the great love of God to turn even your most painful situations into experiences of joy.

When you know and experience the great love that God has for you, it changes everything. I want you to know this love. I want you to experience this love. Oh, how I want you to be embraced by this love.

God loves you.

This book is my effort to help you understand and experience that love.

Your story is different from mine. I told you what God has begun to do in my life so that you could have a vision for what he will do in yours. God has you on a journey to experience the embrace of his great love. The hard news about this journey is that it is likely to begin in a dark, sad, and lonely place. But God is leading you out of this darkness, sorrow, and isolation into the brightness and joy of his great love for you. This journey into God's heart of love is one I want us to take together.

Great love defines God's essence and will transform your existence.

If you understand this sentence, you will understand how this book will progress. In the chapters that follow, I will begin by showing you God's character of infinite love and then explaining how he extends that love to you in acts of care I refer to as his embrace. After I help you answer some practical objections some have about God's love, I will show you how God's great love changes everything about you.

God loves you.

It really is true. And because that is true, it means all the joys and trials you will ever experience are leading you directly into God's embrace of infinite love. I've shared with you a portion of my own experience, and in the pages ahead I will introduce you to other men and women who have experienced this same embrace of love.

I'll share these stories in order to show you how you can experience the same love of God they did. I invite you to grasp this book as if you are taking my hand and let me lead you on a journey to discover the great love of God. This journey will be wonderful. In fact, it will be more than wonderful. I promise you, being embraced by the love of God will be the most wonderful thing that has ever happened to you.

CHAPTER 2

God Is Love

God is love.

1 JOHN 4:8, 16

*I*n the very back of a very small book at the very end of the New Testament appear three words that change the world. These words will change your life. The words are so important that every reality you have ever faced, every pain you have ever confronted, and every hope you have ever cherished absolutely depends on them. The words were written by a man named John. The words are *God is love*.

Those words mean that knowing God requires knowing he is the very definition of love. Those words don't mean knowing God requires knowing he believes love is really important. The words don't mean knowing he is a God who does loving things. They don't even mean knowing God requires having a personal experience of his love.

Those things may be true and important, but they are less significant than the point John is making. Knowing God requires knowing that God, in his very essence—at the core of his being—is the exact definition of love. This is what it means when the Bible says *God is love*.

Is is a very definitive word. When used regarding a person, it describes what they are like. It defines the nature of their existence. This description and definition can be somewhat trivial at times. You can say, "Connor is cute." A statement like this lets you know what Connor is like at a surface level, namely, that he has an appearance that is adorable.

But the description and definition of what a person is like with the powerful word *is* can also be incredibly weighty. You can say, "Connor is kind." This lets you know at a more profound level what Connor is like. It relates the nature of his heart, and you know that he is a person who has a warm regard for others that shines out of his personality. John is giving us a profound insight into who God is and what he is like when he says *God is love*. To say that God *is* love makes love a defining attribute of God.

Love is not God's only attribute. God *is* other things. The same John who says God is love also says that God is light, referring to God's righteousness (1 John 1:5). Jesus refers to God's nonphysical nature and says God is Spirit (John 4:24). The author of Hebrews affirms the justice and judgment of God when he says God is a consuming fire (Hebrews 12:29).

Throughout the Bible, God is also described as merciful, gracious, powerful, and holy—among many other important descriptions. In fact, regarding his attribute of holiness, many have described holiness as the only attribute of God that is repeated three times. Twice in Scripture incredible angels are heard shouting, "Holy, holy,

holy is the LORD" (Isaiah 6:3; Revelation 4:8). This is gloriously true, and we should never ignore anything that is true about God, especially when it is repeated.

In the New Testament, John twice describes a defining attribute of God. When he defines who God is, in the very nature of his being, he does not say God is justice. He does not say God is holiness. He does not say God is wrathful. He says that *God is love* (1 John 4:8). And then, as though we didn't catch it the first time, he repeats, *God is love* (1 John 4:16).

Stop and think about that a moment. The words *God is love* should shock us. The statement "God is . . ." could conclude with any word imaginable. But the word John chose—and chose twice—the word that he wanted to sink deeply into our hearts was that God is *love*.

If you are to experience the great love of God in a new and fresh way, you need to know the God who shows you this love. And the fact that *God is love* means that when you experience his love, you are not experiencing something foreign to him. You have not encountered an add-on to his personality. Love is not a thing God picked up along the way. It is not a skill he had to learn. When you experience God's love for you, you are experiencing something that comes from his very nature. Love is in God like heat is in fire. If you take heat out of the fire, you lose the fire. If you take love away from God, you no longer have God.

Knowing God as he is requires knowing that *God is love*. If you have a conception of God that does not include love as a defining attribute, then you don't know God. You worship a god that does not exist. You bow to an idol. If you are ever to be found in God's loving embrace, it requires knowing that *God is love*.

THE STRUGGLE TO EMBRACE GOD'S LOVE

Experiencing the embrace of God's love requires more than knowledge. Many people confess the truth that *God is love*. This is not enough. God's love must matter to you. You must be changed by it. God's love must grip you. The knowledge that *God is love* makes a demand of each one of us. It requires that we grow in that love. This book is for everyone, because each of us needs to grow in our understanding of the love of God. But several kinds of people find it particularly challenging to embrace the reality that *God is love*. You may be one of these kinds of people.

The first kind of person is someone who is hurting. This is a person who has experienced hatred and pain from someone who was supposed to love her. It could be a spouse, a parent, a child, or a deeply loved friend who failed to love her in return. This failure of love is painful, one of the most damaging betrayals any person can ever experience. People wounded in this way can find it easy to take the pain they feel and tell themselves that love always works that way and always ends in pain. Because one person could not be trusted to love well, nobody can be trusted to love well—not even God. It is hard to embrace the truth that *God is love* when someone has violated our trust with a profound failure of love.

This distrust is understandable. Love is not supposed to disappoint. You are supposed to be able to depend upon the love of another. It is devastating when this turns out not to be true. This devastation is even worse when the failure of love comes from someone in authority over us.

Authority figures like parents, bosses, and mentors woo us with the attraction that they are trustworthy. We believe we can trust them because they make us think they care for us. We trust leaders who we believe love us. That bond of loving trust is one of the most powerful forces on earth. When we discover that a trusted authority has misled us and does not care for us as we thought, it not only damages our trust of them; it damages *us*. Not only does it impact our relationship with them; it radiates out to every relationship we have.

In another sense, however, this distrust is unreasonable. The failure of one person's love does not mean that all people will fail to love us. Perhaps you experienced the pain of a cruel father who mistreated you. That does not mean that other people do not have good dads who loved them well. The cruelty you may have experienced from your wife does not mean there are not many men married to wives defined by kindness and gentleness.

What is true for our relationships with other people is even more true for our relationship with God. Every human being you know will fail to love you well, but God never will. The failure of the love of others can do nothing to change the perfection of God's love. Ask God to give you fresh eyes to see his love and to place your trust in him. He will answer you. I want to help find his answer in the pages ahead.

Another kind of person who finds it hard to understand the great love of God is the brainiac. This is the heady person who studies the Bible thoroughly, takes doctrine seriously, and even pursues advanced degrees in theology. Too much emphasis on love makes this person uncomfortable. He wants the truth, and an emphasis on love makes him uneasy. Not sappy or emotional, he has seen too much biblical truth be corrupted or ignored in an effort to emphasize love. He is frustrated when sentimental efforts to portray the love of God distort it beyond biblical recognition.

Heady people, like hurting people, have a point. Anything true can be harmful when it is stretched beyond its biblical bounds. There is always a risk that well-intended people will take a concept, fail to think in a biblical context, develop a misunderstanding, and then cast their misunderstandings as the truth of God.

Christians have certainly done this with the doctrine of God's love. Some have taken silly, sentimental, and sinful versions of love and presented them as God's love. It is the worst kind of idolatry to start with an image of love developed outside the Bible and parade that counterfeit as the real thing.

Yet heady people should also be the first to acknowledge that there is an infinite difference between a sinful distortion of the character of God and a thoroughly biblical presentation of his love. Those who most love the truth should be most motivated to emphasize what the Bible says about God's love. If nervousness about another's presentation of divine love leads heady people to overlook or minimize biblical truth, then they will have become a mutation of the same disease they diagnose in others. A biblical approach to truth requires affirming that *God is love.*

Another kind of person who needs to grow in their understanding of the love of God is the romantic. Romantics crave the adventure and emotional experience of feeling love. They long to pursue the burst, the thrill, and the rush that accompanies the emotion we call love.

There is nothing wrong with the exhilarating emotions of love. We will talk more about our emotions later. Yet there is a danger when we separate the passionate emotions of love from the concrete truths of love and the tangible actions of love. In their pursuit of divine love, romantics must learn to pursue more than mere feelings.

A final example of the kind of person who needs to grow in their understanding of love is the selfish person. Not many people willingly admit they are selfish, but most of us have selfish instincts when it comes to love. We are selfish in our understanding of love when we think real love is all about us. We demand that people love us by doing what we want, the way we want, when we want, as often as we want. This selfishness is, in fact, the hateful opposite of love (1 Corinthians 13:5).

The God of great love will never behave toward us in ways that encourage hatefulness. In fact, our selfishness is what makes us most blind to God's tender acts of loving care. Our selfishness destroys authentic love, and a vision of the great love of God is the only remedy for the wound.

GROWING IN GOD'S LOVE

Everyone needs to grow in God's love. Whether you are a hurting person, a brainiac, a romantic, selfish, or just one of the countless billions in need of a fresh embrace of God's love, you must grow in your understanding that *God is love*. Your understanding of the great love of God must rise to the next level.

Growing in maturity begins as we come to the Bible and trust God to use his truth to stretch our understanding to reflect the true size of his love. You mature by allowing the words of Scripture to challenge you and move your heart and your desires to a deeper, better place than you have been before. Your personal experience of God's loving embrace will only be mature when it matches the description of love that we find in God's Word.

Growth in our biblical understanding of God's love is the focus of one of the most significant prayers recorded in Scripture. The apostle Paul had a burden on his heart that the people of God would grow in their understanding that *God is love*. And this burden is obvious when we read his heartfelt prayer to the God of love.

For this reason I bow my knees before the Father, from whom every family in heaven and on earth is named, that according to the riches of his glory he may grant you to be strengthened with power through his Spirit in your inner being, so that Christ may dwell in your hearts through faith—that you, being rooted and grounded in love, may have strength to comprehend with all the saints what is the breadth and length and height and depth, and to know the love of Christ that surpasses knowledge, that you may be filled with all the fullness of God. (Ephesians 3:14–19)

This prayer presents three breathtaking realities.

First, you already have the love of God. Paul is praying for and writing to Christians. He knows these followers of Christ encountered God's love when they first came to faith in Jesus. He talks about Christians as those who are rooted and grounded in love. If you are already a Christian, you already know and are connected to the love of God.

Second, our real encounters with God's love are incomplete encounters. Paul prays that those rooted and grounded in love would have God's strength to comprehend the breadth, length, height, and depth of that love. Paul prays this prayer for all God's people because he knows that a fantastically greater, four-dimensional awareness of God's love is available to each of us.

This glorious awareness of love takes nothing less than the power of God to move us to enjoy and experience it. This is why Paul prays. Wherever you are in your walk with God, whatever you think you know about God, and whatever religious experiences you have had, there is more of God's love for you. Your current experience of his love is incomplete.

God's love is so great and your ability to contain it so small that there is always more of it for you to see, know, grasp, and experience. Paul prays for us to have power to know this love. This is a prayer God will answer because he loves to empower his people to experience more of his love.

Finally, even though Christ grants all of us some measure of the love of God and though it is certain we will experience more of this love, the Bible is clear that the journey of growing to know the love of God will never be fully complete. Not now. Not ever. Paul prays that we would know the love of Christ that *surpasses knowledge*.

It is astounding that Paul prays for us to know this love even though it is more than we can ever know. Even though it is possible to know love in increasing measure, God's love will always exceed our created capacities. We have all of eternity to grow in our knowledge of the love of God, yet we will never exhaust the fullness of that love.

This is exhilarating. The love of God is something you already have, it is something you will get more of, yet it is something you will never fully know. Knowing the fullness of the love of God is a destination at which you will never fully arrive. There is more love in God than there is knowledge in you.

Imagine being able to eat all you want of your very favorite food for as long as you wanted without ever getting full or gaining weight. Never filling up would mean there would never be any limit to your ability to experience countless new delightful bites of the food you most cherish. This is how it is with the love of God. Since you will never have exhaustive knowledge of the love of God, there is no limit to the new, delightful, and surprising joys you will discover as you grow in the knowledge of God's love.

You can start the gloriously endless journey of growing in God's love right now. And it is not a journey you make alone but something God wants for all his people throughout history. When Paul prays that we would grow in our knowledge of the love of God, he prays that we would do this *together with all the saints*. For all of human history, God has been working to lead people to a greater understanding that he is the God of great love. Such maturing into the love of God happened in the life of John—the very man who gave us the words *God is love*. You need to know his story.

JOHN'S STORY OF GOD'S LOVE

John was born over 2,000 years ago into an established family with a fishing business profitable enough to afford servants (Mark 1:20). John's dad was Zebedee, and his brother was James. Jesus called these brothers the "sons of thunder" (Mark 3:17). We cannot know for sure whether James and John were sons of an angry and volatile man or whether these character traits marked James and John. What is clear is that the violent language of thunder somehow characterized the brothers, leading us to believe their family life was not always a place of peace, tranquility, and love.

John's family was faithful and religious, so John would have been brought up to be a good Jewish boy. He was raised studying the Hebrew Bible, believing in the existence of God, and learning about God's holiness, righteousness, and justice. He was surrounded by a community of other faithful Jews who worshiped and prayed in the synagogue. John grew up expecting a Messiah, God's anointed king, who would come and redeem God's people.

And then one day John *met* the Messiah.

It happened while John was working with his dad and brother. When Jesus walked by and called John into his service as one of the original twelve disciples, John immediately obeyed and followed. For the next few years, John walked with Jesus, listened to him teach, watched him heal, and experienced his care. John became one of Jesus's closest followers and was included by Jesus in the inner circle of three disciples with Peter and John's brother James. Even within this group, John was special. He alone was known as the disciple Jesus loved (John 21:20–24). John sat closest to Jesus during his final meal before his execution (John 13:23–25) and was given charge of Jesus's mother when the Lord was no longer able to care for her on earth (John 19:26–27).

John received close, personal instruction from Jesus. He learned directly from God in the flesh. Prior to meeting Jesus, he had learned *about* God by studying the words of Moses. Now he would come to know God in person as he lived with the Word made flesh. Living with Jesus changed John. The years-long encounter with the Messiah expanded his knowledge and stretched his understanding of the true character of God.

After Jesus had died, risen from the grave, and ascended into heaven, John had years to reflect on all that God had revealed to him. He thought about who God was revealed to be in the pages of the Bible and then remembered all that God had revealed in the person of Jesus. He remembered all he had seen and heard from Jesus and everything that Jesus had taught him about who God really was. As John reflected on his life lived with Jesus . . . something happened to him.

For the first time in his life, John understood who God really was. The disciple Jesus loved was struck by the true character of God. John had experienced the loving embrace of God in person. And in the rapture of that embrace, John sat down by the light of an oil lamp and wrote the most profound truth he knew, a truth that had changed his life and that he knew would one day change yours. The truth was that *God is love*.

The reality of God's love was not new, only John's experience of it. Throughout all time and in every situation, God's great love has remained constant. Throughout endless ages extending into the past and through an eternity of future moments, God's loving nature remains.

The problem is not that God has failed to demonstrate that love. *God is love.* Because *God is love,* he must demonstrate that love. The problem is not God's showing but our seeing. The purpose of all of human history and your entire life is to see what has been clearly shown all along, what John saw: that *God is love.*

The personal embrace of God's love changed the man who had been known as a son of thunder into a man known forever afterward as the apostle of love. The change Jesus wrought in John also answers an important question you already should have asked by now.

At the beginning of this chapter, I observed the truth that *God is love* is revealed at the back of a very small book at the end of the New Testament. The pressing question you should ask is, If the truth that God is love so defines God himself, then why must we wait until the very end of the Bible to hear it taught with such explicit clarity?

The answer to this pressing question is found in Jesus. To be clear, there is biblical teaching about the nature of God's loving character all throughout the Bible, which we will explore throughout this book. And yet we wait for the obvious and repeated statements that *God is love* until John writes them at the end of the Bible. You have not seen the greatness of the love of God until you have seen Jesus. The dazzling fullness of God's love is found only in encountering him.

God did not become fully visible to humanity until he was made known by Jesus Christ in his life on earth (John 1:18). John got a closer picture of Jesus than anyone else, and he was uniquely equipped to lead the rest of us to fully discover the great love of God.

Then John did something amazing and wonderful. After he experienced the embrace of God's love, he wrote that truth down because he wanted you and me to see and experience its reality just the way he did. God delights to display his love through others who have experienced it. He showed the world God's love through John's experience of it. He is showing you his love right now through my experience. And throughout the rest of this book, I want you to encounter God's loving embrace so that, having experienced it yourself, you would then be able to share that love with others.

The problem is not in the showing but in the seeing. The problem is not a matter of the existence of God's love but our experience of it. The rest of this book, like the rest of your life, is about seeing and experiencing what God has clearly shown. It is about encountering a crucial part of God's own nature. It is about seeing with your own eyes and showing with your own life that *God is love*.

CHAPTER 3

A Vision of God's Love

He has wondrously shown his steadfast love to me.

PSALM 31:21

Great love inspires glorious language. That's the lesson you learn from the life of David. He was a man who was so greatly loved by God and who returned God's love so devotedly that he has been known throughout history as a man after God's own heart (1 Samuel 13:14). David expressed both his love for God and his experience of God's love by writing the poetry of the psalms. His entire life was an experience of embrace after embrace of the great love of God. And one of those encounters happened in the strangest of places and in the darkest of times.

David was the great king over God's people, but his reign fell on hard times. His own son Absalom schemed to displace him and take the throne in his place. The climax of the crisis found the rightful king of Israel running for his life, away from a son who wanted a throne more than a father.

David had barely escaped the palace. Fleeing the city of Jerusalem, many of his followers had abandoned him, and his own son was trying to kill him. He was weeping, barefoot, and covered his head both to display his grief and to conceal his identity. For a man who had known many trials, this was a low point. Then, in the midst of his desperation and tears, in the chaos of heartbreak and pain, in his deep loss and shame . . . something happened to David. God embraced him in the arms of divine love (2 Samuel 15:25; 17:14; Psalm 31:7).

David knew he had encountered divine love. He had experienced God's embraces many times before and had often described them with beautiful, poetic language. Many forget that in addition to being a king, David was also an artist who composed songs, sang, played instruments, and wrote poetry. David's poems comprise a large portion of the Old Testament book of Psalms and easily make him the most famous poet in human history. David knew how to turn a phrase, and his gift of writing never shone more bright and clear than when he was talking about the love of God.

David's pen was a fountain flowing with joy and wonder at the great love of God. In one place, he wrote, "All the paths of the LORD are steadfast love and faithfulness" (Psalm 25:10). This is a glorious truth that is gloriously expressed.

In talking about God's love, David could have said that the Lord always behaves in a loving way. That would have been a straightforward way to communicate something true, but David wanted to communicate the love of God in striking, visual, and beautiful ways. In another psalm, David describes God's love as a physical presence encompassing him: "Steadfast love surrounds the one who trusts in the LORD" (Psalm 32:10).

When he wants to declare how wonderful God's love is, he portrays a majestic vision of a powerful bird flying to protect its young, "How precious is your steadfast love, O God! The children of mankind take refuge in the shadow of your wings" (Psalm 36:7). David doesn't just tell us it is good to trust in the love of God, he says,

> I am like a green olive tree
> in the house of God.
> I trust in the steadfast love of God
> forever and ever. (Psalm 52:8)

David uses the image of a crown to communicate how God showers his people with love. God, he says, "crowns you with steadfast love" (Psalm 103:4).

David uses beautiful words to paint a striking picture of the great love of God—word pictures that help us as we grow in our own understanding of God's love. Word pictures can enable us to understand unfamiliar concepts by comparing them to something we have known or experienced. To describe the beauty of the ocean to someone who has never seen it, I might say that the blue of the water stretches to the horizon, as though the sky were turned on its head. David used word pictures because he knew that God's love is unfamiliar to most, and he wants us to understand and see what he knew. As real as God's love is, it can be hard for us to see, to experience, and to understand. God kindly gives us language about his love that is connected to imagery we can grasp.

At other times, a word portrait conveys the weight of emotion where plain language fails. The descriptive power of a word picture or metaphor reaches beyond the literal expression of truth to convey the depth of emotion, the profound nature of the experience, or the power of the reality you want to express. If I want my wife to know the depth of my love for her in a note I send to her on Valentine's Day, it is more effective to say, "Lauren, my love for you is higher than the mountains and deeper than the oceans" than it is to say, "Lauren, I love you a great deal."

Having encountered God's love in such a powerful way, David reached for exalted language and beautiful words to convey his experience and understanding of God's love. His heart was full to bursting, and he needed grand images to translate this love into words others could read. God's love is so wonderful and incomprehensibly glorious that the constraints of literal language must be transcended with the visual power of symbolism to faithfully describe it.

We have already talked about the concrete expression that God *is* love. As this book unfolds, we will further unpack additional details about the definition of God's love, what I've expressed as his commitment based on who he is to delight in you, to give you wonderful things, and to protect you from harm.

The work of this chapter is not that of concrete definition, but rather the work of exalted expression—using words to portray God's love like an artist paints a picture. God's love is bigger, grander, and far more beautiful than any literal depiction could convey. The glorious metaphors we find in Scripture ignite our imagination and protect us from thinking small thoughts about the great love of God.

Great love inspires glorious language, and David marshaled all his gifts of expression and artistry to help you and I get a taste of the great love that had mastered his soul. We will follow David, and his words will take us deeper into the heart of God and enable us to experience a warmer embrace of God's great love.

GOD'S LOVE IS LIKE A FAITHFUL SHEPHERD

Before David was a famous poet-king, he was a shepherd (Psalm 78:70–72). Few of us today understand what is involved in being a shepherd, but David spent the early part of his life becoming an expert at herding and caring for sheep. The three responsibilities of a shepherd were to be present with the sheep and ensure they stayed together, to tend the sheep and guarantee they had everything they needed, and to defend the sheep against the many dangers they faced—from cliffs to ferocious animals. The work of a shepherd required great diligence since a shepherd was often alone, and the shepherd had to keep a constant eye out for sheep straying from the flock. Such diligence took precedence over the shepherd's own need for sleep and personal care.

The work of a shepherd is the work of love. Jesus makes this connection in John 10:11–12 when he draws a distinction between the two kinds of people who watch over sheep. He contrasts the true and good shepherd who sees danger coming and lays down his life for the sheep to protect and defend them with one not invested in the flock—the hired hand—who flees when he sees danger and leaves the sheep to care for themselves. The second caretaker is in it for the money and will only care for the sheep to a certain point. A good shepherd cares about the sheep, not his own personal gain.

While his brothers were at home hoping to be selected as the next king of Israel, David the faithful shepherd diligently cared for his family's flocks (1 Samuel 16:10–11). When his older brothers were hiding in their tents from Goliath, the great enemy of God's people, David, who was still too young to fight in the army, did the hard work of shepherding (1 Samuel 17:12–15). When enemies like bears and lions came to attack the sheep, David fought them off, risking his life to protect the precious flock (1 Samuel 17:34–35).

David knew another faithful shepherd when he saw one, and that is what he saw when he experienced God's loving care and kindness. The most famous line David ever wrote captures this glorious truth in Psalm 23:1, "The LORD is my shepherd; I shall not want." With this powerful word picture, David tells us what God's love is like. David knows he is a needy sheep, and the Lord is a loving shepherd who will meet his needs and keep him from want. David knew the shepherd tended the sheep, protected the sheep, and stayed with the sheep. When he says God is his shepherd and he will never experience want, he expresses his conviction that God's love perfectly meets every one of his needs.

The idea that God loves us like a shepherd may seem abstract in our modern economy far removed from caring for animals that we depend on for our livelihood. Understanding the three responsibilities of a shepherd can help you know how this metaphor communicates God's love for you. Whenever you face physical needs for food or money, David reminds you that the Lord is your loving shepherd who provides all the tangible resources you need in life: "He makes me lie down in green pastures. He leads me beside still waters" (Psalm 23:2).

In the dark times of your life when you need forgiveness, comfort, or solace, David reminds you that your God loves you as a shepherd: "He restores my soul" (Psalm 23:3). Even when you face threats, taunts, or the danger of living in a world full of enemies, your heavenly shepherd loves you with his perfect protection:

> Even though I walk through the valley of the shadow
> of death,

> I will fear no evil,
> for you are with me;
>   your rod and your staff,
>   they comfort me.
> You prepare a table before me
>   in the presence of my enemies. (Psalm 23:4–5)

Finally, David reminds us that you and I have never really been alone no matter how lonely we've felt. You have a diligent, faithful, and loving shepherd who will never forsake you but will stand with you throughout this life and into the next, "Surely goodness and mercy shall follow me all the days of my life, and I shall dwell in the house of the LORD forever" (Psalm 23:6).

As a shepherd himself, David knew all of us need a shepherd who loves us. David wrote Psalm 23 to let you know you have someone who loves you that way. David communicates a personal vision of God's great love with this powerful word picture. But it is not the only picture he developed to communicate the profound nature of God's love.

GOD LOVES LIKE A GREAT DAD

David also wrote of the love of God by comparing it to the love a father has for his son. The image of a shepherd might not strike as close to your heart as it did for David, but every person on the planet has a dad. Though some fathers did not show up for us or failed to show us love, we all understand something of that relationship. Perhaps that is the reason why the image of fatherhood is so regularly used to describe God's love.

David says, "As a father shows compassion to his children, so the LORD shows compassion to those who fear him" (Psalm 103:13). Fatherhood helps us understand something true about God, namely that the same loving compassion a human father has for his children reflects the love God has for his people. Many other places in Scripture use this same metaphor. The apostle Paul calls God's people "sons of God" (Galatians 3:26) and "beloved children" (Ephesians 5:1). The author of Hebrews says, "God is treating you as sons" (Hebrews 12:7).

The apostle John tells us, "See what kind of love the Father has given to us, that we should be called children of God" (1 John 3:1). These brief words contain two shocking statements you must not miss about God's great love. First, God wants you to *see* his love for you. This is God's great desire. He places his love right in front of your face so you can't miss it. We are faithful followers of God when we fill our hearts with longing to see, grasp, and understand his love more deeply. That's a prayer God is always happy to answer.

The second thing from this verse that shocks us is that when God wants us to see what kind of love he has for us, he stuns us by calling himself our father and naming us his children. God tells us that the love he has for us is like the love of a great dad—a love filled with wisdom, mercy, and kindhearted compassion for his kids. What comes into your mind when you think of a great dad?

I think of Dick Hoyt and his relationship with his son, Rick. Rick was diagnosed at birth with cerebral palsy after a significant complication blocked the flow of oxygen to his brain and made it impossible for Rick to walk. When Rick was fifteen, he wanted to participate in a race to benefit a paralyzed student in his school, but because Rick could not physically run by himself, he needed his dad to push him in a wheelchair.

Rick's dad agreed, and that first race began a decades-long athletic partnership that came to be known as Team Hoyt. This father-son pair has since competed in hundreds of athletic events, including a run across the United States in forty-five days. They have competed in triathlons with Dick running with his son in a wheelchair, riding with his son on a specially designed bike, and swimming while pulling his son along with a rope attached to a special raft. When Rick could not be present to train for these races, Dick would run with cement bags to simulate his weight.

Why would Dick run when no one was chasing him? Why compete in races doing the work of two people instead of one? After their first race together, Rick looked at his father and said, "Dad, when I'm running, it feels like I'm not handicapped." Dick did what he did because he was a dad who wanted to lavish his son with love.

The great God of heaven and earth wants you to know that his great love for you is like the love of Dick Hoyt for his son. The difference is that God's love for you is perfect. It never fails.

Perhaps you have memories of your dad wrapping his arms around you or putting your face in his hands, staring in your eyes, and telling you how much he loved you. Maybe you sat snuggled at your dad's side while watching a movie or resting in the park. You may have had a dad who carried you on his shoulders, pushed you on the swings, or tossed you high in the air as you laughed so hard your sides hurt. I really hope you had a dad like that. If you did, you need to know that God in heaven loves you more than what I've described, not less. God's love is more pure, more perfect, and longer lasting.

If you never had an earthly father who showed you love or if you had a person in your life who hurt you, you can still know the love of a heavenly Father who loves you with a love that is better than anything you might have missed. You can know that love because God tells you over and over that he loves you like a great dad loves his kids.

GOD'S LOVE IS LIKE THE EARTH AND CLOUDS

These word pictures describe what God's love for you is like. But another set of metaphors paints an even greater portrait of God's great love for his people. These word pictures portray not what God's love is like but how much of his love there is. David says, "For your steadfast love is great to the heavens, your faithfulness to the clouds" (Psalms 57:10; 103:11; 108:4). Don't just skip over those words. Experience a wondrous vision of the vastness of God's love for you!

When I was a little boy, a few boards colored with crayons and nailed into a tree trunk transformed a redbud tree into a place of wonder we called the rainbow tree house. My cousins and I would lie on our backs and stare at the sky through the beautiful blossoms of that tree. We imagined what it would be like to float up to the clouds, which we thought must be edible and, we were sure, tasted like marshmallow cream. Unfortunately, we could never be certain because no matter how high we climbed or far we stretched, we were never able to touch those glorious, puffy clouds floating so high above us in the bright blue sky.

Look out your window and stare up into the sky. Try to imagine what it would take to reach the clouds drifting high in the air. Go to the roof of a tall building, climb to the top of a high tree, hike to the summit of the greatest mountain, and stretch your hands into the air. You will not be able to reach those lofty clouds perched high in the heavens. Let the vastness of the sky fill your mind and your heart.

David wrote those words thousands of years before air travel at a season in his life when he was isolated and in danger in a remote mountain range. Imagine David high in the mountains, thinking about the enduring love of God while others hated him and plotted against him. He gazed into the sky, and though he was seated atop a high mountain, the distance was barely closed between himself and the clouds in the vast expanse above.

As he looked at those faraway clouds, he was struck to the heart by how much love God had for him. When David sought to communicate how much love God had for him, he painted the picture of God's love reaching to the unreachable clouds. There is more love in God for you than there is space between your tiny existence on earth and the clouds seated high in the heavens.

But there is more.

The Psalms also say, "The earth, O LORD, is full of your steadfast love" (Psalm 119:64). Marvel at this! I have traveled all over the world from the United States to Switzerland, from England to Brazil, from China to South Africa, from Israel to France, from Germany to Egypt, and many, many other places. When you travel as much as I have, you learn how colossal the world is. It takes a tremendous amount of time, energy, and money to get to all the places you could possibly go. And when you consider the geographical expanse of the entire globe, I have visited just a tiny fraction of the world.

As big as the earth is, the Bible says that God's love fills up the world! This means that when God loves you as a shepherd or as a dad, he loves you with an immensity that can only be compared to the earth itself. God has more love for you in his perfect divine heart than there are places to visit in the whole wide world.

God describes his colossal love with a very special term we find in the Old Testament, the word *hesed*. The translators of your Bible often use several different terms to portray this Hebrew word including mercy, steadfast love, and lovingkindness. *Hesed* is a delightful word used hundreds of times in Scripture to explain God's great love for his people. Just one important example is in Psalm 136:1. We read, "Give thanks to the LORD, for he is good, for his steadfast love endures forever." The verse begins with a command: *be grateful* to God because he is good. Then the psalm depicts his goodness as a great love for his people that lasts forever and ever. We should be the most grateful people because we know the God whose goodness is found in his eternal love for his people.

This eternal love is a glorious miracle. The love of every diligent shepherd and the love of every great dad will come to an end. Death brings a conclusion to the lives of the most loving people you have ever met. But God never dies. He lives forever. For as long as he is alive, his perfect love for you is stretching to the sky and filling the earth. The love of God for you lasts as long as God himself.

These three dramatic portraits of God's love are just a small fraction of the pictures God uses throughout Scripture to communicate what his love is like. God communicates his great love in dozens of other powerful word pictures. God's love is described as the reign of a righteous king over his precious people (Revelation 1:5). God's love is described as a strong right hand that protects you from danger (Isaiah 41:10). God's love is like the rescue of a mighty warrior (Revelation 19:11–16). It is like the tenderness of a mother bird caring for her young (Deuteronomy 32:11). His love is solid like a rock (Isaiah 26:4). God's love is like the satisfaction of bread for a hungry person (John 6:50–51) and the oversight of a careful gardener in a vineyard (John 15:1–7). God's love is illuminating like light (Psalm 27:1) and close like a friend (Isaiah 41:8). It is gentle like a lamb (Isaiah 53:7) and strong like a fortress (Psalm 9:9). God's love is like the safe shelter of a refuge or tent (Psalms 27:5; 61:4), it defends like a shield (Psalm 3:3; Proverbs 30:5), and it covers you like a hiding place (Psalm 32:7). God's love is selfless like the payment of a ransom (Matthew 20:28) or an animal sacrifice (John 1:29). More portraits exist of God's love in the Bible than we could unpack in a lifetime! Yet one final metaphor remains, and it is so important and powerful that our survey of the portraits of God's love cannot be complete without it.

GOD'S LOVE IS LIKE A
FAITHFUL HUSBAND

When God wants us to know the depth and intimacy of his love for us, he uses the image of a husband loving his wife. The prophet Jeremiah describes God's relationship with his Old Testament people of Israel and says,

> I will make a new covenant with the house of Israel and with the house of Judah, not like the covenant that I made with their fathers on the day when I took them by the hand to bring them out of the land of Egypt, my covenant that they broke, though I was their husband, declares the LORD. (Jeremiah 31:31–32)

God's relationship with his people, according to Jeremiah, is like the relationship of a husband and a wife.

But this metaphor goes far beyond saying that God is a loving husband. The biblical vision of God as husband portrays God as a husband who is full of love for his *sinful* wife, a woman who refuses to love him in return. Jeremiah says that God is a faithful husband to a wife who repeatedly breaks her covenant and vows of fidelity. The marriage metaphor communicates a God who loves with faithfulness and commitment *even though* his marriage partner is faithless and unloving.

The most elaborate unfolding of this metaphor in the Bible is found in the Old Testament book of Hosea. Hosea was a prophet called to reveal God's love to his people, and God used Hosea's life to visibly demonstrate that love.

God's call to Hosea occurs in Hosea 3:1: "And the LORD said to me, 'Go again, love a woman who is loved by another man and is an adulteress, even as the LORD loves the children of Israel, though they turn to other gods.'" Here, God's love is portrayed more than that of a loving and faithful husband to a good wife or even the love of a husband whose wife does not love him in return. God's love is portrayed as that of a husband who loves his wife while she openly pursues sexual relationships with other men.

The image of God's love as a husband emphasizes the biblical nature of covenant. Throughout the Bible, God demonstrates his love for his people by entering relationships with them called covenants. The marriage relationship is a covenant agreement, just as God's relationship with his people is called a covenant in Jeremiah 31:32.

A covenant is a relationship based in love with obligations for everyone involved. The Bible portrays God as the member of the covenant who keeps his obligations while his bride fails to keep hers. God's love for his people is like that of a loving and faithful husband whose great love is not returned but hated and rejected by his wife.

This image is especially powerful to me because I have personally known a husband who loved like this—my father. My dad was married to my mom for nearly twenty years, and she mistreated him for most of that time. In God's kindness, by the time my mom died, she had become a Christian, and I was able to know her as a wonderful mom, mother-in-law, and grandmother. But all of those good things happened after she divorced my dad.

While married to him, she was a drunk who was violently abusive, slept around, and made repeated attempts to leave him. Some of my earliest memories of life were watching my dad's futile efforts to love my mom even though she always spurned his love.

When she was drunk, he would help her sober up. When she would threaten to leave, he would plead for her to stay. When she was pregnant with me and my twin brother by another man who didn't want us, he took us as his own and put his name on our birth certificate. Even after she left him, when she was in need, he was always there to offer help.

Decades later, after she had changed and it was too late to restore their marriage, she lost her battle with cancer. My dad came to the family visitation at the funeral home and wept over her casket covered in a beautiful spray of daisies that he paid for because he always knew they were her favorite.

My friend, God's love for you is like that. In your disobedience, you have spurned him and embraced another, but he has never abandoned you. You have betrayed him and rejected him, but he has never stopped loving you. You have hated and despised him, but he longs for you and desires to be restored to you.

God uses the powerful word picture of a husband in love with his faithless wife because it perfectly pictures his relationship with you. Though you have been faithless to God, he has never stopped loving you. In fact, he loves you right now with that faithful love of a husband even when you have broken his heart with your sin.

THE PERFECT PORTRAIT OF GOD'S GREAT LOVE

As wonderful as these portraits are of God's great love, there is still one portrait of his love even greater, the one drawn for us by his Son, Jesus Christ. He lived a perfect life on earth as the flawless demonstration of who God is. Colossians 1:15 says, "He is the image of the invisible God." The Bible also says that Jesus "is the radiance of the glory of God and the exact imprint of his nature" (Hebrews 1:3). But Jesus is not a word picture or a metaphor. Jesus is the perfect portrait of who God is.

If we want to know what God and his love look like—if we really want to see this love—we must look to Jesus in the Bible as the perfect portrayal of love. Jesus is the great shepherd of the sheep who perfectly cares for his people so that they receive his perfect righteousness and eternal acceptance into the presence of God (Hebrews 13:20–21). Jesus Christ is the true Son of the Father whose life secures the Father's love so that all who believe in him can know God as their own perfect father (Galatians 4:4–7). Jesus is a perfect husband who faithfully loves God's people, his bride, and washes them in his spotless blood so they can be presented to him as a perfect bride (Ephesians 5:25–27).

Images are powerful, striking, and wonderful ways to convey God's love for his people. But they do not convey that love perfectly. The only perfect portrayal of God's love comes not in a picture but in a person. That person is Jesus Christ, and it is only through him that we can experience the perfection of God's loving embrace.

CHAPTER 4

God Delights in You

$\mathcal{CO}$

The LORD takes pleasure in his people.
PSALM 149:4

What comes into God's mind when he thinks about you is one of the most important things about him. You can begin to understand what God thinks about you in the story of a young boy who was the precious son of a very rich man. As the boy grew up, he became disenchanted with his father, with following his rules, and with living in his house.

One day the boy worked up the nerve to request the immediate receipt of his own massive share of his father's inheritance. It was a breathtaking request since asking for his inheritance meant he wanted his father's possessions without his father's presence. The boy was saying he wished his dad was dead. Yet even more breathtaking than the son's request was the father's response. The father granted his son's outlandish request and gave him the inheritance.

Flush with cash, the boy moved far away and began living a wild and crazy life. He engaged in every activity a wicked heart craves but usually cannot afford. He caroused at parties and frequented bars. He burned through cash buying every toy and trinket he desired. He filled up on booze, did all the drugs he could find, and slept with as many women as he wanted. He was having a great time. Until the money ran out.

His loss of money changed everything. The friends and the women who had once hung on his every word disappeared, and he began to see that they liked his money a lot but had never really cared for him. The liquor, the parties, and the spending sprees that had once brought him such joy were now the source of his ruin. Without a penny to his name, he was forced to care for pigs to stay alive, eating the scraps of food left over from feeding them. Where he had once enjoyed lavish and expensive food, he now stared with longing at the slop the pigs were served. More than any of these problems, he missed his dad.

The boy had once imagined life away from his father's house as something wonderful—a chance to finally be free of rules and obligations. Reality was far different. Hardship is a brutal instructor, and the boy learned his lessons well. He began to see that freedom is not worth much without love.

It is easy to attract "friends" when you give them what they want, but nothing can replace the unconditional love of a father. The boy remembered life in his father's house, how much food was available, and how kind his dad had been to him. He now looked with longing at what had once seemed restrictive. He wanted to go home.

One day, he determined that he would face the consequences of his actions, committing himself to the long journey home where he would look his father in the face and confess what a terrible son he had been. He would swallow every ounce of pride, admit he was wrong, and beg to be restored to his father's house as the lowliest of servants. It would be shameful and humbling—one of the hardest things he had ever done—but he knew it would be worth it just to be near his father again.

As the boy returned home, he discovered something he hadn't counted on. Since he left, his father had spent every day looking for him, longing for him, and desiring his return. Each day he would stand at the edge of his property, checking the horizon for a glimpse of his returning son. Then, one day, the father couldn't believe his eyes as he saw a familiar silhouette in the foreground of the setting sun. He had seen that figure many times and would know it anywhere. It was his son! His boy had returned home!

Flooded with love and in full view of his servants, this wealthy and dignified man broke into a run. He approached his smelly unwashed son, locked him in an embrace that lifted him from the ground, and covered his filthy face in fatherly kisses. His son was home, and his heart was filled with joy.

The son, who had been ready to feast on humble pie and accept the judgment of his father, never expected that great and wonderful love would prioritize the restoration of relationship over punishment for sin.

GOD DELIGHTS IN YOU

Jesus told this story of a rebellious, prodigal son to reveal a crucial dimension of God's love for his people. As you think about the connections between this story and the heart of God, I want to ask you an important question: When God thinks of loving you, what comes into his mind?

We often think of God's love in terms of our experience of that love. But I'm asking you to consider God's experience of his love for you *before* you ever encounter that love yourself. What does it mean *to God* when he looks at you and declares, "I love you"? To answer this question, we must look deep into the heart of God.

God's love is his commitment, based on who he is, to delight in you, to give you wonderful things, and to protect you from harm. This definition describes God's loving character, his loving attitude toward you, and his loving actions for you. God's loving character has been the focus of earlier chapters. How God behaves toward you is the subject of future chapters. This chapter is about God's attitude toward you. The definition of God's love articulates the emotional experience in the heart of God.

When most people talk about love, they often are describing an emotional experience. They are talking about that moment when feelings of love swell in the heart. And this emotional experience of love also happens in the heart of God. When the Bible talks about God's great love, it includes God's *feelings* of love for his people. God's great love certainly includes more but never less than this emotional experience of compassion and affection for you.

If you want to understand the true nature of a person's love, it is not enough to examine his behavior since people behave out of all sorts of motivations on a continuum from cruelty to kindness. In order truly to know the love a person has for you, you must know what is in his heart. And this is true for God as well. Your experience of the love of God begins by understanding and experiencing God's heart concerning you. To know God's great love for you, you must understand what is in his mind when he thinks of you.

The wonderful news is that God has told us in the Bible what he thinks of us. Consider just a few of the things God says in the Bible about how he feels toward his people. The Lord says that his people are his treasured possession: "The LORD has declared today that you are a people for his treasured possession, as he has promised you" (Deuteronomy 26:18). The Lord says that his people are precious to him: "You are precious in my eyes, and honored, and I love you" (Isaiah 43:4). The Lord draws his people near with love that will never end: "I have loved you with an everlasting love" (Jeremiah 31:3). This great love of God for his people will never end: "The steadfast love of the LORD never ceases; his mercies never come to an end" (Lamentations 3:22).

The Lord speaks of his love for his people with the most passionate intensity: "How can I give you up . . . ? How can I hand you over . . . ? My heart recoils within me; my compassion grows warm and tender" (Hosea 11:8). The Lord takes joy in his people: "The LORD your God is in your midst, a mighty one who will save; he will rejoice over you with gladness" (Zephaniah 3:17).

These are just a few examples, and the Bible is jammed with many, many more. Here is my best effort to summarize in a few sentences what hundreds of texts say:

> As one of his children, God freely sets his affection on you so that you are his precious possession. God honors and treasures you. He is for you. God has compassion on you. God rejoices over you. He delights in you. God is filled with longing for you and pursues a closeness of relationship with you that he will never cut off, even though you sin.*

---

* It is my desire to have every word of this be anchored in the truth of the Bible. If you are interested, you can consult the following Bible passages that support each assertion in

These words tell us the longings in the heart of God toward his people. To simplify it even more, we can say that God's internal experience of love for you is one of delight. *God delights in you.*

If our minds could ever fully grasp this glorious thought, it would overwhelm us. I can write it down, but it won't fully capture the awe-inspiring truth these written words are intended to convey: *the God of the universe has fond feelings of affection for you.* Before God ever shows his love to you, he *feels* love for you.

The God of all power who made the world and holds it together feels affection for you. God, who is so glorious in power that from the foundation of eternity he has never had a single need, has an emotional experience of love for you. He delights in you. He longs for you. He desires a relationship with you. God loves you.

This truth is so stupendously, gloriously, and jaw-droppingly amazing that you may have trouble believing it. Perhaps the idea of God having an emotional experience about you makes you uneasy. You may be uncomfortable with that statement because of who you are. As you think about yourself and how sinful and insignificant you are, it might seem wrong that God—a majestic and good God— could have such fond feelings of affection for you.

Or perhaps you are uncomfortable with this idea of God's love

---

the paragraph. God loves you as one of his children (Psalm 103:17; Proverbs 3:12). God's love for you is a free exercise of his will and is not required by any good thing in his people (Deuteronomy 7:7–8). God's love has to do with his own internal affections (Deuteronomy 7:7; 10:15). In his love, God considers his people to be his treasured possession (Exodus 19:5; Deuteronomy 26:18; Psalm 83:3). In his love God honors his people and esteems them highly (Daniel 9:23; Zephaniah 3:17). In his love, God considers his people precious to him (Isaiah 43:4). In his love God has compassion for his people (Exodus 34:6; Psalm 51:1). In his love God rejoices over his people (Deuteronomy 30:9; Jeremiah 32:41; Zephaniah 3:17; Luke 15:6–7). In his love, God delights in his people (2 Samuel 22:20; Psalm 22:1; 62:4). In his love, God has a longing to be close with his people (Hosea 11:8; John 14:21, 23). God never stops loving his people (Exodus 34:6; Numbers 14:18; Psalms 100:5; 106:1; 107:1; 136:1–26; 138:8; Isaiah 54:8; Jeremiah 31:3; Lamentations 3:22). God loves his people in spite of their sin (Psalm 51:1; Hosea 3:1; Luke 15:6–7).

because of who God is. You know of his great majesty and power, you have some understanding of his limitless perfection, and you appreciate his commitment to his own glory. That awareness makes you uneasy when you think about him having an intimate relationship with you.

Whoever you are and whatever concerns you have, I hope to convince you that the great love of God for you is true. It will not be enough to believe in this kind of love simply because you want it to be true. Nor should you reject it because you struggle with it. You must believe it because the Bible says it is true. God's heart of love is filled with affection for you, and he has revealed that truth in Scripture to prove that it is true. It is not too good to be true. God delights in you.

GOD'S EMOTIONS

Some people are uncomfortable with the idea that God has emotions. But Scripture portrays God not only having emotions but strong ones. And we must not forget that God is the source of our emotions. He created us, and the emotional life of human beings is one of the ways we bear his image. The Bible says that God gets angry (Psalm 7:11), sad (Genesis 6:6), and happy (Psalm 104:31)— just to name a few of the ways he is described using emotional language. Of course, God also loves, taking emotional delight in his people (Psalm 18:19).

If we are inclined to believe it is wrong for God to experience the emotional delight of love, it is because we have learned what we believe about feelings from our human experience of emotions instead of the Bible. As people, we have different, sinful expressions of love. Some people get caught in the strong waves of affection and their emotions blind them from seeing the truth about someone. Or people we love may have behaved toward us with fickle affection where their "love" was constantly changing in a painful on-again, off-again cycle. We may have seen a sinful failure to love in our own heart where we refused to have affection for those we are supposed to love.

God, however, is spotlessly perfect. He never sins in his emotional life. God's love is never blind to the truth (Hosea 3:1), never grows cold and changes (Micah 7:18), and never fails to love that which is lovely (Psalm 138:8). Because God is perfect, his internal experience of love is perfect. God's love is not initiated from factors outside of himself. What he feels for us is unstained by sin and selfishness, and so it is the perfect and universal standard for the emotion of love.

GOD'S GLORY

It is clear in Scripture that God's ultimate motivation for everything he does is his glory. More than anything else, God is committed to honoring himself as God whenever he does what he does. The prophet Isaiah speaks for God and says,

> For my own sake, for my own sake, I do it;
>> for how can my name be profaned?
>> My glory I will not give to another. (Isaiah 48:11)

Because God is God, he prioritizes his name and his glory above everything else (Ezekiel 36:22–23).

The language often varies when the Bible describes this reality. Sometimes the Bible says God acts for the sake of his name, for the sake of his goodness (Psalm 25:7), for the sake of his righteousness (Isaiah 42:21), for the sake of his holy name (Ezekiel 36:22), for the sake of Christ (2 Corinthians 12:10), or simply for the sake of "the name" (3 John 7). But it is all the same.

When God acts, his chief motivation is that of advancing his own glory. This important truth is not something for us to skip over. It lies behind the nervousness some people may feel when we speak of God's affection for his people. The Bible's emphasis on God's glory makes some people nervous to highlight love in a way that seems to place people in competition with God himself for priority of affection.

But the Scriptures build a tension on this topic because just as there are passages that describe God's motivation for his actions as the pursuit of his own glory, his name, and his righteousness so there are numerous passages in Scripture that describe God's actions as being for the sake of his people.

God promises to spare an entire city for the sake of fifty righteous people or even ten (Genesis 18:24, 32). God delivered his people from Egypt for Israel's sake (Exodus 18:8). God promised Solomon he would not punish him for the sake of David (1 Kings 11:12). God anoints Cyrus king for the sake of Israel (Isaiah 45:4). Jesus sanctifies himself for the sake of his followers (John 17:19). Jesus died and rose again for the sake of everyone who would ever believe in him (2 Corinthians 5:15, 21). There are many more examples of passages just like these.

What are we to do with this tension? On the one hand, some passages of Scripture describe God as being motivated by his interest in his own name and glory. On the other hand, different passages describe God as motivated by his interest in and love for his people. The good news is that this tension is not contradictory. The presence of a primary motivation does not rule out the existence of other motivations as well.

My desire to take my wife to dinner to honor her and give her a night out does not contradict my own desire to spend an evening with her myself. God's activity toward his people is motivated by complementary desires. He desires to advance his own glory, and he desires to delight in his people. Far from being at odds with one another, the two work together in unity. Whereas we often experience our desires in tension and competition with one another, God's desires work together.

The Bible itself puts these two motivations together. There are biblical examples of God engaging in one activity both for his sake and for the sake of his people. When Hezekiah's bold prayer for an extension of life is answered, God promises to defend the city for God's own sake and for David's (2 Kings 20:6). God spares Jerusalem from destruction for the very same reason (Isaiah 37:35). The apostle Paul is willing to suffer various trials in ministry not only for the sake of Christ but also for the sake of Christ's people (Colossians 1:24).

We can make the case even stronger. Not only is it true that the Bible puts together God's desire to work for his own sake and his desire to work for the sake of his people, it also never separates these two realities. In every biblical example where God is described as engaging in an action for his own sake, the activity is always done as a demonstration of love to his people. When God acts for the sake of his glory, it is always to show love to his people—whether to grant righteousness (Psalm 23:3), to forgive their sins (Psalm 25:7, 11; Isaiah 43:25; 48:9; Ezekiel 36:31–33), to provide guidance (Psalm 31:3), to give aid in a difficult season (Psalms 79:9; 106:8; 109:21; 143:11; Jeremiah 14:7; Ezekiel 20:9), to share his law (Isaiah 42:21), to listen to our prayers

(Daniel 9:17, 19), or to send messengers around the world with the good news of Jesus Christ (Acts 9:16; Romans 1:5).

This is stupendously good news. God's desire for his own glory and honor is never at odds with his love for you. When we are told that God is love, this means that he knows how to do whatever he does for his own glory *and* out of profound delight and affection for you. God's love for his people never conflicts with his pursuit of his own glory. The great God of heaven pursues his own glory through the path of love for his people, "Rise up; come to our help! Redeem us for the sake of your steadfast love!" (Psalm 44:26).

GOD'S INTEGRITY

One of the reasons God's loving delight in his people is tied inextricably to his own glory is that God does not just love his people for fickle, changing reasons. His love does not depend on our love for him but on his promise to love. The prophet Isaiah proclaims to God's people, "'With everlasting love I will have compassion on you,' says the LORD, your Redeemer" (Isaiah 54:8). This is a promise guaranteeing that God's internal disposition of delight toward his people will never end—it endures everlastingly.

The moment God makes a promise to love his people, God's loving nature is bound up with his righteous commitment to be the God who keeps his word. God never lies (Numbers 23:19; Titus 1:2; Hebrews 6:18). So, when God promises to love his people forever, we can be confident that he will keep his word. His own integrity depends on it.

When God keeps his word to love his people, he will not keep his word grudgingly:

> I will make with them an everlasting covenant that I will not
> turn away from doing good to them. And I will put the fear of
> me in their hearts, that they may not turn from me. I will rejoice
> in doing them good, and I will plant them in this land in faith-
> fulness, with all my heart and all my soul. (Jeremiah 32:40–41)

The God who commands us to love him with all our heart and
soul makes a promise to love us with all his heart and soul. God's
delight in his people is not grudging and temporary but enthusiastic
and eternal. This glorious, faithful, and steadfast love preserves the
integrity of God, who has promised to love his people.

LOVING SINNERS

The most significant challenge to God's strong affection for his
people is our sin. The Bible is clear that all of us are guilty of sin
(Romans 3:23). Our experience bears out the reality of this biblical
truth. Every person alive has disobeyed God: we have told lies, gos-
siped, committed adultery, erupted in anger at our family, looked at
pornography, stolen from our work, cheated on our taxes, mistreated
our spouse, taken the Lord's name in vain, behaved hypocritically,
and a hundred and ten other things.

Because God is completely perfect in his righteousness, these sins
have a disastrous impact on our relationship with God and separate
us from him (Isaiah 59:2). It is right and normal to question how
people who are guilty of such sin could be anything but repulsive to a
God who is defined by flawless righteousness.

This is why we must understand the rest of the story we read
earlier in this chapter. If you recall, the son was returning home from

his wicked excursion bearing all the marks of a sinful binge: he would have been filthy, his breath may have stank of liquor, he may still have had traces of lipstick on his neck from a night with a prostitute. None of that stopped his father from embracing him with joy. Luke 15:20 says, "While he was still a long way off, his father saw him and felt compassion, and ran and embraced him and kissed him."

The father wrapped the rebellious boy in an embrace of fatherly affection. The father's extravagant and affectionate display of love—running to his lost boy, embracing him, and kissing him—was motivated by something greater than the boy's sin. Jesus says the father felt strong emotion and deep compassion. Jesus wants us to know that the father was moved with great love for his sinful son—despite his rebellion and betrayal.

The "prodigal son" is a parable, a story told to communicate a deeper truth. In this parable, you and I are that prodigal son and the father is God. Jesus wants us to see that the great love the father has for his boy is a picture of the great love of God for you.

Though you have sinned, disobeyed, turned your back on God, and spurned him, he has never stopped loving you. He has compassion on you, strong feelings of affection for you, and delight in you. Jesus told the story of a faithful father embracing a sinful son because he wanted you to know this is how God treats you. The father embraces the prodigal because God embraces you. From the bottom of his everlasting heart, God loves a sinner like you.

If you wonder how something so glorious could be so true, you are not alone in asking that question. And the answer to that question is that God has another child besides you. The eternal Son of God became a human being and was born as the baby we know as Jesus of Nazareth. That child never sinned—living a perfect life (2 Corinthians 5:21; Hebrews 4:15). One of the most repeated descriptions of Jesus Christ in the New Testament is that he is God's beloved Son (Matthew 3:17; 17:5; Mark 1:11; 9:7; Luke 3:22; John 3:35; 5:20; 10:17; 2 Peter 1:17). Because Jesus was perfect, God the Father perfectly delighted in him. And this delight—the unchanging, eternal love that God the Father feels for God the Son—causes something miraculous to happen when you put your trust in the life, death, and resurrection of Jesus Christ to forgive your sins. Jesus explains in John 16:27, "The Father himself loves you, because you have loved me and have believed that I came from God." God wants people to love and trust his Son, and the amazing miracle of God's great love for us is given when we believe in Jesus.

Oh, how you need to hear what Jesus says when he speaks to his Father and explains the nature of his great love: "The glory that you have given me I have given to them, that they may be one even as we are one, I in them and you in me, that they may become perfectly one, so that the world may know that you sent me and loved them even as you loved me" (John 17:22–23).

And loved them even as you loved me.

Did you see that?

Even as you loved me.

When you trust in Jesus, God loves you with the same love he has for his own perfect Son. Forever and ever, the perfect God of heaven and earth will shower his great love on you, delighting in you as he delights in Jesus himself.

Take some time for that to settle in.

It is overwhelming. It is astounding.

It is God's great love for you. And it is available through Christ alone.

CHAPTER 5

God Gives You Wonderful Things

I will praise your name,
for you have done wonderful things.
ISAIAH 25:1

God's love gives.

I am writing these words at Christmastime. It's the early hours of the morning in our home, and all is dark and quiet. The only light in the room where I sit shines from our beautifully bright Christmas tree in the corner. Stuffed under the tree are dozens of sparkling gifts, each one a token of love for the precious members of my family.

The names on the packages are the names of the people who mean the most to me in the world: Lauren, Carson, Chloe, and Connor. No one in my family is lacking gifts under our tree because there is no one in my family that I don't love. When you love someone, you give them things. The Bible teaches that God does the very same thing.

God's love gives.

Many biblical words communicate the meaning of God's love. We have already talked about *hesed*, a Hebrew word communicating God's loyal and steadfast love. There are several other words as well, but the most noteworthy is the Greek word *agapē*. This term conveys another unique aspect of the great love of God. Millions of people who do not know the first thing about the original Greek language of the New Testament have heard and used this word countless times. It is a term that communicates something of the richness of God's love in his generous compassion to his people.

One of the most helpful words in the Bible communicating God's great love for his people is a common word that we tend to overlook—the word is *gift*. This is a word God uses to communicate the powerful nature of his love. The idea that love gives is true even when the specific word, gift, is not used. Whenever God is providing, bestowing, presenting, allotting, conferring, imparting, granting, or otherwise sharing good things with his people, he is giving them a gift. God shows love whenever he gives gifts.

The fact that God's love gives is an essential part of understanding the love of God. God's love is his commitment based on who he is to delight in you, to give you wonderful things, and to protect you from harm. God loves you not just by delighting in you but also by giving you wonderful things. God's love—by definition—gives, and it gives you more than you might imagine.

GOD'S LOVE SEEN IN GOD'S GIFTS

Jesus talks about God's commitment to give good gifts to people in response to their prayers. "Ask, and it will be given to you," he promises, and then reaffirms, "For everyone who asks receives." (Matthew 7:7–8). Jesus proves this commitment to give good gifts to people is based in love by asking a question about a father's commitment to his son: "Which one of you, if his son asks him for bread, will give him a stone? Or if he asks for a fish, will give him a serpent?" (Matthew 7:9–10). His point is that you can pray for things with the expectation of receiving them because of the way fatherly love works. Loving fathers give good gifts to their children. When dads love their kids, they never withhold good things, and they never bestow bad things. Jesus's point, however, is much stronger than this.

Jesus knows—and you know too—that every good father on earth is still imperfect and sinful. They struggle to show love and often fail to give the very best gifts. That struggle does not make the principle untrue, however. Even imperfect fathers know how to give good gifts. This leads Jesus to his greater point: "If you then, who are evil, know how to give good gifts to your children, how much more will your Father who is in heaven give good things to those who ask him!" (Matthew 7:11). Your Father in heaven is not beset by the sins and weaknesses of human fathers. God's love is perfect, making his ability to give good gifts infinitely superior to any human father's.

In his teaching on bread, stones, fish, and snakes, Jesus never uses the word *love*. Yet Jesus talks about love by talking about gifts. Love's presence is indicated by love's action. The perfect father in heaven gives good gifts to his people.

God's love gives.

One of the most shocking commands in the Bible also demonstrates this truth. The command to love your enemies (Matthew 5:44) jars and challenges us because it runs contrary to the way we naturally want to respond to mistreatment. Our world responds to hate with more hate. When wronged, we want revenge.

If Jesus is going to be taken seriously in reversing the norm, he needs to provide a powerful justification for it. And he does. He tells us we must respond to our enemies with love because this makes us like God (Matthew 5:45). God loves by giving gifts to people *who do not love him*, "He makes his sun rise on the evil and on the good, and sends rain on the just and on the unjust" (Matthew 5:45). Anyone can be nice to people who are nice to them. It is easy to show love to people who love you in return (Matthew 5:46–47).

God does not behave like this. God gives gifts of sun and rain—not just to the people who love and follow him but to people who hate and deny him. God gives to his enemies because he loves them. This kind of love demonstrates God's perfection: "You therefore must be perfect, as your heavenly Father is perfect" (Matthew 5:48). The fullness of God's perfection is not seen merely in his giving gifts but in giving those gifts to people who reject him.

Scripture is soaked through with the reality that God's love gives. Ezra the priest knew that God loved him when he *gave* him favor in the sight of King Cyrus (Ezra 7:27). It is the delight of God's heart to *give* the kingdom to his people (Luke 12:32). God the Father loves the Son and has *given* all things into his hand (John 3:35). Jesus says the greatest example of love is when someone *gives* his life for another person (John 15:13). God loved us and *gave* us eternal comfort and good hope through grace (2 Thessalonians 2:16).

Our understanding of the giving nature of love is further expanded by the wonderful word *blessed*, which communicates the idea of gifts being bestowed through divine favor. Jesus calls Simon blessed because God has *given* him the revelation that Jesus is the Christ, the Son of the living God (Matthew 16:17). Believers in Jesus are called blessed because of the *gift* of the inheritance granted by the father (Matthew 25:34). In the Beatitudes, Jesus explains that the poor are blessed because they are *given* the kingdom of God, the hungry are blessed because they are *given* satisfaction, those who weep now are blessed because they are *given* joy, and those who are insulted and criticized are blessed because they are *given* a great reward in heaven (Luke 6:20–23). All the various terms in Scripture for God's gifts portray his commitment to shower his people with wonderful things.

You know you have received God's loving embrace when he gives you wonderful things. One crucial path to experiencing God's embrace of love is learning to identify and recognize God's gifts. Whenever you receive a divine gift, you are encountering God's love.

I want to help you learn to identify God's gifts through the story of one of the most blessed men in history, King Solomon of Israel. Solomon received an overwhelming abundance of gifts from the hand of God. God wrapped his arms of perfect love around this remarkable man and made his life a demonstration of the great love of God. There are four categories of gifts that God gave to Solomon, and these guide us to understand and appreciate his great love for you and for me.

IN LOVE, GOD GIVES YOU PROMISES

Solomon was the prince of Israel, the son of King David. Being born into this privileged position was only the beginning of Solomon's remarkable life, which culminated in his installation as king of Israel. Solomon's reign was the result of a promise to David that he would always have a descendant on the throne.

After Solomon had been installed as king, he remembered the promise God had made to his father, King David: "Now therefore, O LORD, God of Israel, keep for your servant David my father what you have promised him, saying, 'You shall not lack a man to sit before me on the throne of Israel'" (1 Kings 8:25). But notice how Solomon recalls God's promise. He unpacks the heart of God in giving it: "O LORD, God of Israel, there is no God like you, in heaven above or on earth beneath, keeping covenant and showing steadfast love to your servants who walk before you with all their heart; you have kept with your servant David my father what you declared to him" (1 Kings 8:23–24). Solomon knows that God's promise demonstrated his steadfast love. God loves, and so he gives. And here, God gives a promise.

God's promises are extraordinarily loving gifts to his people. Think of a promise as a bridge. Bridges link two points, often to overcome some barrier, like a river or a canyon. Promises serve a similar purpose. God's promises link God's delight in his people to the gifts he gives to his people, overcoming any barrier that prevents them from receiving them. Before God gives gifts, he promises those gifts to the people in whom he delights. These promises are themselves precious gifts of love because nothing requires God to make promises to people. He makes them freely, often overcoming barriers that stand between him and his people.

We see promises in Solomon's life, but these precious gifts of love do not just benefit him. Far from it. Promises apply to all of God's people. They are for you as well. Consider a tiny sample of the promises God gives to you: God promises that he will be with you (Deuteronomy 31:6; Isaiah 41:10); that he will give you guidance when you are confused (Psalm 32:8); that when you pray he will hear you (Psalm 55:17). When you are in pain God will comfort you (Matthew 5:4); you will have power to put away sin and live righteously (Romans 6:14); when you are tempted he will provide a way of escape (1 Corinthians 10:13); your faithfulness will eventually produce fruitfulness (Galatians 6:9).

In all these ways and more, God could have just given the gift when it was required. For example, every time you are tempted, God could be faithful to provide the gift of escape right when you need it without ever telling you he would provide it. Eventually, over the course of your life, you would be able to look back and see, whether you took it or not, every time you were tempted that God provided a way to escape from the temptation. But this is not the way God does it. He does not love us by merely giving the gift of escape from temptation.

He loves us even more by giving the gift of the promise, telling us in advance that such a method of escape will always be available. This is a superabundant love, a down payment on the gifts that will be available in the future. You can face the future, with all its unknown trials, confident in the love of God for you to provide a path of escape from any temptation. God not only lavishes us with gifts but grants us the promise of those gifts in advance.

IN LOVE, GOD GIVES EVERYTHING YOU NEED FOR LIFE

The most important event in Solomon's life happened after he had been installed as king. God appeared to Solomon in a dream and made a breathtaking offer: "Ask what I shall give you" (1 Kings 3:5). The God of the universe spoke to his child and demanded the privilege of showering a blessing on him. Why? God desired to show his love to Solomon.

Solomon recognized this as the loving embrace of the one who had shown great love to his family: "You have shown great and steadfast love to your servant David my father . . . You have kept for him this great and steadfast love and have given him a son to sit on his throne this day" (I Kings 3:6). He recognized God's gifts of love in the past, and now he responds to the divine invitation, saying, "Give your servant therefore an understanding mind to govern your people, that I may discern between good and evil, for who is able to govern this your great people?" (1 Kings 3:9).

God was delighted that Solomon had asked for discernment rather than for long life, riches, or honor. So, he granted his request for wisdom and then gave even more than he had asked: "I give you also what you have not asked, both riches and honor, so that no other king shall compare with you, all your days" (1 Kings 3:13). We will discuss God's loving gift of wisdom shortly, but for now, let's look at the additional gifts God gave—the gifts given to Solomon that he did not request. These gifts point us to the loving, generous, and compassionate heart of God. God gives and gives, and then gives more. In this case, God gives tangible gifts.

The gifts of God we tend to dwell on the most are the ones we need to live life on earth. These are tangible gifts we can see, hear, touch, feel, spend, and enjoy every day of life. These gifts are more than important—they are required. They are also wonderful. The tangible gifts God gives to Solomon are a window into the ones he gives to you.

God Gives the Gift of Life

Solomon knew he had already received God's loving gift of life in God's promise to David (1 Kings 3:6). The gift of life is one that God has already given to you and to everyone who has ever lived. "He himself gives to all mankind life and breath and everything" (Acts 17:25). God gives the precious gift of children: "He gives the barren woman a home, making her the joyous mother of children" (Psalm 113:9). God gives the gifts of sun and rain that make life possible (Matthew 5:45). Nothing exists in this life that does not come through God's loving provision (1 Timothy 6:17).

No matter who you are, if you are reading these words, you are alive. You are breathing, seeing, hearing, and thinking. You are the valued creation of the God of great love. Your life is a gift of incalculable worth from God himself. There is no requirement that you must live, but here you are. God's loving gift of life allows the enjoyment of all God's other gifts.

God Gives the Gift of Honor and Stature

Another gift God gives is honor and stature. This has to do with your reputation and what people think of you. God promised to give Solomon this gift so that no king would compare with him in honor (1 Kings 3:13). You do not have to be a king to have a good reputation. In his love, God caused Joseph to grow in favor (Genesis 39:21). He gave the Israelites favor in the eyes of the Egyptians at the time of the exodus (Exodus 11:3). God gave the gift of a favorable reputation to Samuel (1 Samuel 3:19–21), David (2 Samuel 5:10), Uzziah (2 Chronicles 26:14–15), Hezekiah (2 Chronicles 32:23), Ezra (Ezra 7:6), Daniel (Daniel 1:9), and many others. In fact, anyone who has received the blessing of honor and favor has received it from the Lord (Psalm 37:18–19; Luke 1:52).

It may surprise you to see this listed as a gift from God, but consider how important your reputation is. After satisfying a basic need to survive, what people think of you may be the most important thing about you. Your reputation matters everywhere you go and in whatever you do. What people think of you is crucial in your ability to live peacefully in your home. Whether you have close personal friends or not depends on your reputation. With a good reputation, you can get a great job, but with a bad reputation you'll hardly be able to get any job at all. The truth is, we spend a massive amount of energy in our life obsessing over what people think of us, rejoicing over the people who think well of us, and brooding over the people who do not.

Your reputation is so important that knowing it is a gift of God's love will free you from much trouble and worry in life. Earlier, I mentioned the years of ministry pain that led to the writing of this book. One of the more difficult aspects of that struggle was the terrible treatment I received from people who were behaving in sinful ways toward me and my family. Among the most painful experiences of that mistreatment were the terrible lies people spread about me. The lies were especially painful because they were started by people who took no interest in the truth but in destroying me and my reputation. The absurdity of the lies did not keep them from being repeated and believed, seriously damaging what many thought of me.

At one point during this period, some dear friends of mine from around the country reached out to me and my wife and expressed concern about the damage to my reputation. They had known me for years, loved and respected me, and had come to believe that I should leave our church before dishonest people ruined my reputation beyond repair and destroyed my potential for future ministry. Lauren and I took their counsel very seriously, as you always should when wise people who love you give you advice. Ultimately, however, we decided to stay at our church.

There were several reasons for this decision, but one of them had to do with understanding that our reputation was a gift from

God. I knew that anything good about my reputation was a free, undeserved gift of love from my heavenly father. Because any good reputation I have comes from God, sinful people cannot take it away. Ultimately, all that matters is what God thinks of me. Lauren and I decided to remain as an act of faith, trusting God to give us whatever he wanted for a reputation rather than worrying about what other people think of me.

You do not have to be bound by the thoughts, judgments, and opinions of others. You can live in freedom as well and eliminate years of striving by giving up the lie that your reputation comes from your effort. Instead, embrace the truth that your reputation is a loving gift from your heavenly Father. What he thinks about you is ultimately what matters.

You don't have to stress, lie, manipulate, or even try to cover your weaknesses. You need only to rest in God's loving desire to grant you his favor and know that only he can ultimately determine what people will think of you. Your goal is to live for him, not to receive the applause of people or to escape their criticism.

The Gift of Financial Resources

God made good on his promise to give riches to Solomon and made him one of the wealthiest men in history (1 Kings 3:13; 10:14–22). This same gift comes from God to any person throughout history who has amassed financial resources. This is true for the richest men in the Bible including Abraham (Genesis 24:35), Isaac (Genesis 26:12–13), Jacob (Genesis 32:9–10), and Job (Job 1:10; 42:10–17). Any needy person who receives financial resources has received that gift from God (Psalm 68:10). This reality is also true for you (2 Corinthians 9:8–10). Any financial resources you have are a gift to you from God himself.

Embracing money as an expression of God's love releases you from worry and stinginess. These sins come from a belief that we will not have enough money and things will be bad for us. But believing money is a gift of God's love helps us to trust in *him* to provide what we need even when we would like more money. Fight the lies of stinginess and worry with the truth of God's love. Your ability to care for yourself and give to others is fueled by God's commitment to care for you.

But all of this raises a crucial question. How do we account for the difference between people who have little financial resources and those who have many? If God's love is seen in his gifts, does this mean that God loves rich people more than those who are comparatively poor? Does it mean that having great financial resources indicates greater blessing or love from God? Are financial trials a mark of God's disfavor? I will say more about this in chapter 7 when I talk about God's love and our suffering. For now, we can observe that God does not obsess over wealth the way greedy people do. Wealth is just one of the many gifts God gives, and we should never evaluate God's love for anyone based on his bestowal of one gift, but we must grow in our ability to see his love in the combination of gifts he provides.

IN LOVE, GOD GIVES YOU EVERYTHING YOU NEED TO PLEASE HIM

This leads us to a broader understanding of how and why God gives because God gives yet another category of gifts that are unlike the ones you see and spend. These gifts are just as real, but they address our life through the spiritual realm of our existence. These gifts are not for your body but for your soul, though they do affect our bodies.

God's intangible gifts may be invisible, but they are just as real and often far more important than the tangible gifts we often obsess about. These gifts enable God's people to live lives that honor and please him. In 2 Peter 1:3, God promises, "His divine power has granted to us all things that pertain to life and godliness." God provides everything we need to live for him and have a relationship with him. This kind of spiritual gift was the focus of Solomon's request for wisdom.

On the most important night of Solomon's life when God asked to grant him a gift, he asked for the spiritual gift of wisdom (1 Kings 3:5–9). Solomon did not seek a tangible gift but instead asked to be anointed with the gift of wisdom. He requested an understanding mind to discern between good and evil. He wanted the ability to accomplish the work God gave him. God gave him such vast wisdom that it became the source of his fame throughout the world and throughout history (1 Kings 3:12, 28; 4:29; 10:24).

The gift of wisdom may be the gift people associate most with Solomon, but it was not his only spiritual gift. He also received the gift of hearing the word of God. Before Solomon obtained the gracious gift of wisdom, he received a glorious invitation through the audible voice of God. In a breathtaking display of love, God's Word came to Solomon (1 Kings 3:5). And then, compounding the wonder, Solomon was given another spiritual gift, the privilege of God hearing him in return. Solomon was heard. God listened to the voice of Solomon, and "it pleased the Lord that Solomon had asked this" (1 Kings 3:10).

You have received these very same gifts. You have the privilege of hearing from God in the pages of the Bible, the recorded speech of God (2 Peter 1:21). When we encounter God's Word in the Bible, we have an even greater assurance of the truth than if we heard God with our own ears (2 Peter 1:16–19). God's written word to his people today is every bit as real, every bit as clear, and far more comprehensive than anything Solomon received. This is a gift of God's great love to you.

God also gives wisdom to his people today. God gives wisdom for you to hear his voice and to follow him in faith (John 10:27). God gives wisdom and guidance for you to understand the Word he has given (Ephesians 1:17–18). God gives you wisdom about how to obey him when what you really want to do is disobey (Psalm 119:34), wisdom about what to say when you are in trouble (Matthew 10:19–20), wisdom when you are confused (James 1:5), and much more (Psalms 25:4–5, 12; 27:11; 48:14; 51:6; 73:24; 119:27; 143:8, 10; Proverbs 2:7; Luke 1:79).

God also hears his people today as he heard Solomon. One of the most tender demonstrations of God's love occurs in prayer, as God hears his people by granting them an ear (Psalms 39:12; 54:2; 55:1; 88:2; 102:2; 141:1; 143:1). When God's people pray to him and ask him for things, he often responds by giving what they have asked, as he did for Solomon. Of course, there are also times when he responds in a way that is different than they asked, and the things requested are denied. It can be difficult to embrace the truth that God expresses his love to people by giving them good gifts when, at times, they are denied that for which they pray the hardest.

This way of thinking fails to understand how love is expressed. One of the great joys of my life is living with my children, who ask me for things all the time. A while ago, my daughter asked me if she could go out with some of her friends, and I told her yes. Not long after that, she asked about going out again, and I said no. When I said yes to her first request, I knew the group, knew the parents, and understood what they would be doing. When I said no to her second request, I had much less information about the group and was less comfortable with what they were going to do. In each case, my daughter received a different answer, but my motivation was unchanged. I love her and want wonderful things for her.

It is the same with God. We must not evaluate God's love for us by whether he provides his children with everything they want but by the fact that we have his ear. He always hears us and then responds in love to our requests. Our response is to trust him and remember that he is good and has our ultimate good in mind.

We can only scratch the surface of the spiritual expressions of God's love. There are many, many more. We have been blessed with every spiritual blessing (Ephesians 1:3). God grants his people spiritual fruit to reflect his character (Galatians 5:22–23) and gifts from the Holy Spirit to serve him (1 Corinthians 12:1–11). All these gifts point to the central gift God gives, God himself.

The great men of the Bible expressed deep concern that they would be removed far from God. Faced with the terrible sin he committed with Bathsheba, David pled with God, "Cast me not away from your presence" (Psalm 51:11). On the opposite side of this concern is the great hope in Scripture that God's people would enjoy the presence of God in a deeply close relationship of love. The prophet Ezekiel declares God's promise of great love to his people: "You shall be my people, and I will be your God" (Ezekiel 36:28). God longs for the time when his people will be together with him forever (Ezekiel 43:9). When Ezekiel prophesies about the end of time, he points to a magnificent city where all of God's people will live with him forever, and the name of the city is "The Lord Is There" (Ezekiel 48:35).

God's love gives.

God wants to give you wonderful things. And when God wants

to give you the very best thing, he must give you the gift of himself. This is exactly what he gives to all those who know him. You get his words, you get his wisdom, and you get his ear. But all these are in the service of getting the best gift of all—the gift of God himself.

IN LOVE, GOD GIVES YOU EVERYTHING YOU NEED TO LIVE WITH HIM FOREVER

One of the most repeated realities in all of Scripture about God's great love is that it endures forever (1 Chronicles 16:34, 41; 2 Chronicles 5:13; 7:3, 6; 20:21; Psalms 100:5; 103:17; 106:1; 107:1; 118:1–4, 29; 136:1–26; 138:8; Jeremiah 33:11). Because God's loving character endures forever, his loving gifts are meant to as well. Yet even though God's love endures forever, human sinfulness limits our experience of those gifts.

When God made the human race, he gave incredible gifts of physical provision and close intimate fellowship with one another and with God. Yet the people God made misused his gifts. They sinned. In their sin they put their desire for God's gifts above the giver and sought to place themselves above God. This terrible reality disrupted the equilibrium of the entire cosmos and introduced the horrifying reality of death, placing the ultimate limitation on the ability of people to enjoy God's loving gifts. The great love of God endures forever, but physical and spiritual death has ended our ability to experience that love forever.

In spite of all the gifts of love he received, Solomon turned his back on God. Like every other sinner, he was frustrated with the gifts God had given and became greedy for things the Lord had not granted. If Solomon is famous for anything other than the gift of wisdom he received, it is his lustful greed for the women he sinfully enjoyed. Listen to this assessment of Solomon's life: "Did not Solomon king of Israel sin on account of such women? Among the many nations there was no king like him, and he was beloved by his God, and God made him king over all Israel. Nevertheless, foreign women made even him to sin" (Nehemiah 13:26).

God's lavish gifts of love are no protection against sin. What was true of Solomon is true of each one of us. Regardless of the number of blessings we receive our sin ensures that we will always love the gift more than the giver. Our hearts constantly grasp for gifts we have not been granted.

Solving this problem requires another gift from God, the gift of his forgiveness. Forgiveness is God's gift to overlook our sins and release us from the penalty of death that our sins deserve. Solomon knew he needed this gift: "By steadfast love and faithfulness iniquity is atoned for" (Proverbs 16:6). Solomon knew that sin needed to be addressed and that addressing that sin with atonement required God's love.

This gift of atoning forgiveness ensures that God's people can experience God's great love forever. The gift of eternal life allows you to avoid all judgment for your sin and to pass from death to life (John 4:14; 5:24). Eternal life allows us to enjoy God's gifts and to enjoy God himself forever without any interruption.

But this gift of forgiveness and eternal life requires God's greatest gift. The greatest gift God gave to his people is his Son, Jesus. The most famous verse in all the Bible declares, "For God so loved the world, that he gave his only Son, that whoever believes in him should not perish but have eternal life" (John 3:16). God demonstrates his love for the world in the precious gift of his one and only Son. This truth is repeated throughout the New Testament. Paul says, "The life

I now live in the flesh I live by faith in the Son of God, who loved me and gave himself for me" (Galatians 2:20). In another place, Paul says that "Christ loved us and gave himself up for us" (Ephesians 5:2). John says, "By this we know love, that he laid down his life for us" (1 John 3:16). God's greatest gift is the gift of his precious Son.

God has given you everything: "Every good gift and every perfect gift is from above, coming down from the Father" (James 1:17). This passage teaches us of the overflowing love of God without ever mentioning the word. Every gift you have ever received has come from him. He has given you life, breath, and all the resources you need to live on earth. He has given you rich and powerful gifts to be able to please him as you follow him as one of his people. He has given you eternal gifts to be able to enjoy him forever. And he has given you all of this through forgiveness when you trust in the most precious gift of all. He has given you the gift of his Son, Jesus Christ, who gave his life for you so that you could enjoy forever the great love of God for you.

CHAPTER 6

God Protects You

He . . . rescued us from our foes,
for his steadfast love endures forever.
PSALM 136:23–24

To make it in this world, you need help. With diseases, natural disasters, economic collapses, corrupt governments, opioid epidemics, global sex trafficking, white-collar crime, invading armies, and gang violence, being alive is dangerous business. The world is not only terrifying, but we are weak. Every person on earth is far more exposed to harm than we usually care to admit. The typical person can't afford to miss a paycheck or two before life comes to a halt. Even the fabulously wealthy and powerful are constantly exposed to the great equalizer of humanity—death.

Regardless of your financial resources and political connections, an invisible virus, one metastasizing cell, or a single misplaced truck on the freeway can bring your life to an abrupt end. Nobody is safe. If you have an ounce of honesty, you'll have to admit that you could never have made it this far in life without some help.

That horrifying reality encourages us to remember God's love, his commitment based on who he is to delight in you, to give you wonderful things, and to protect you from harm. So far, we have looked at God's loving character and God's delight in you. We have also considered some of the wonderful things that God gives you. Now, we will look at the final element of God's love, which is his protection of you. God's love for you means that even weak people like you and me have protection in a world as petrifying as this one.

GOD'S PROTECTION

God protects you. This truth is one of the most obvious demonstrations in the Bible of God's love for his people, and hundreds of examples of this truth exist. Let's consider a few. King David knew God had delivered him from all his enemies and said, "He brought me out into a broad place; he rescued me, because he delighted in me" (2 Samuel 22:20). The gathered people of God sing out to God for rescue, "Rise up; come to our help! Redeem us for the sake of your steadfast love!" (Psalm 44:26). When Hezekiah was sick, and God healed him he declared, "In love you have delivered my life from the pit of destruction" (Isaiah 38:17). Nehemiah faced incredible enemies as he sought to rebuild the wall around Jerusalem, and he pled with God, "Spare me according to the greatness of your steadfast love" (Nehemiah 13:22).

The healing ministry of Jesus delivering people from disease is explained in terms of love and compassion: "When he went ashore he saw a great crowd, and he had compassion on them and healed their sick" (Matthew 14:14). The apostle Paul had great confidence in God's great love to deliver him from the evils of this wicked world: "The Lord will rescue me from every evil deed and bring me safely into his heavenly kingdom" (2 Timothy 4:18). In his love, God protects, guards, delivers, rescues, and saves.

One of the most precious promises of divine protection in all of Scripture comes from the pen of the apostle Peter. Peter discovered the comfort of God's loving protection and wrote, "Humble yourselves, therefore, under the mighty hand of God so that at the proper time he may exalt you, casting all your anxieties on him, because he cares for you" (1 Peter 5:6–7). Peter's promise to God's people emphasizes God's incredible strength to help humble people exposed to danger: *Humble yourselves, therefore, under the mighty hand of God.* God's incredible might encourages us to cast all our anxieties on him because there is no danger that is too great for our God to handle. Peter's promise of protection emphasizes not just God's strength but also his love: *Casting all your anxieties on him, because he cares for you.* God's strength would be slender solace if he did not love us. God's protection is based on his compassion as much as his power. God's love means that he desires to use his limitless strength to defend you.

When Peter promised God's loving protection, he was not extending a pious platitude. Peter rested in this promise because he was repeatedly the recipient of God's protection. Peter knew the embrace of God's great love because God had rescued Peter throughout his life. Peter was devoted to communicating the promise of God's protection precisely because of his own experience.

GOD'S LOVE PROTECTS YOU FROM TROUBLE

We all encounter trouble. The word *trouble* communicates the most general kinds of difficulties we face in life. Trouble is all the terrible stuff you experience without anyone trying to hurt you. When your house floods after a rainstorm, it is not the fault of any particular person—sometimes it just rains really hard. Losing your job in a round of layoffs doesn't mean anyone is out to get you, just that resources are limited in a fallen world. When you're late for a job interview and your car runs out of gas because the broken gauge reported a full tank, it isn't your fault—we just live in a world where everything breaks. In a world full of death and dying, when your parent dies of pneumonia, you won't necessarily be able to find anyone to blame.

The lack of a responsible party does not take the sting out of trouble. Some of the most painful realities you will ever experience are the result of terrible tragedies for which no particular person is to blame. A flooded house can destroy precious heirlooms and family mementos, a lost job can create punishing financial consequences lasting years, and the death of a parent leaves a painful hole in your heart that will remain as long as you're alive.

The terrible thing about trouble is that nobody can escape it. Trouble finds everyone. It has found you before. It will find you again. Trouble also found Peter, but he experienced divine rescue, and he wants you to know that such rescue is also available to you.

Peter found himself in trouble a lot. One example was when his mother-in-law was sick with fever. You might not think a fever is a big deal, but in a world before telehealth, drugstores, and Tylenol, it could be deadly. God protected this woman when Jesus walked into the room and healed her with a touch (Matthew 8:14–15).

On two occasions, Peter was at risk of drowning. The first time was with the other disciples when a massive storm threatened to capsize their boat and end the lives of all on board. Jesus protected Peter and the rest, stopping the storm by saying simply, "Peace! be still!" (Mark 4:39). On a different occasion, Peter was sinking in the sea and cried out for Jesus to save him when Jesus extended his hand and raised him to the surface (Matthew 14:30–31). Each of these are examples of divine rescue accomplished by the miraculous intervention of Jesus Christ himself.

God loves you and will rescue you in the same way. The Bible says of God that he is "the Savior of all people, especially of those who believe" (1 Timothy 4:10). Two truths are taught in this passage. The first is that God is the source of eternal salvation to everyone who trusts in Jesus Christ. But God saves in ways other than extending eternal salvation.

He saves in the way Peter asked to be saved when he was sinking in the sea by sparing the health and safety of all who are in trouble. This is the second truth in 1 Timothy 4:10, that God is the Savior of all people. That you are alive and reading this book evidences that throughout your life, you have been spared from illness, endured disaster, and rebounded after a financial crisis. You have personally experienced the saving protection of God. This protection is a demonstration of God's love:

> As for you, O LORD, you will not restrain
>   your mercy from me;
> your steadfast love and your faithfulness will
>   ever preserve me! (Psalm 40:11)

Reflect on all the dangers, toils, and snares that the Lord has delivered you from. Remember all the pain, the serious illness and injury, the financial pressures, the brushes with death. Consider that you made it through all of them and are sitting here alive today. Then consider that your flight from that trouble was no mere escape. You were rescued by the hand of God in a glorious display of divine love. Consider that and be overwhelmed. Consider that and rejoice.

And that might not even be the best part.

There is a way that God protects you from trouble that you may never have considered before but which is illustrated in Peter's life at a time when he was in serious trouble. In the days of the early church, Peter was the very first preacher, and for his faithfulness he endured jail and a serious beating (Acts 5:40). This beating was terribly severe. Peter would have been placed in a kneeling position naked from the waist up and beaten thirty-nine times using a thick piece of leather with every third strike coming across his chest. It was a serious punishment and might have resulted in death, but God was kind and protected his servant from death.

Peter was painfully aware of his punishment and was thankful that he was spared. What is amazing, however, is all Peter did *not* know. The council that sentenced Peter to a flogging had first wanted to kill him. But Peter was spared death when one man stood during their proceedings and made an appeal for leniency, which won the day. Peter did not enjoy being beaten, but a flogging is better than an execution. The amazing thing is that the council deciding his fate had dismissed Peter from their proceedings (Acts 5:34). Peter was not even in the room when his fate was decided and might never have known how close he came to death had God not used the voice of one man to spare him.

There is a powerful lesson in this incident that is also true for you and me. Perhaps you've been reading this chapter with objections in the back of your mind. As you read about God's loving protection you've been thinking about all the times when it didn't seem like you were protected. You remember the terrible troubles you've endured and wonder where God's protection was in that moment. Why, if God loves you so much, did he allow that to happen? This is a larger question that I'll turn to in the next chapter. But the lesson from Peter's life still stands, encouraging us to think of God's protection not merely in the things you can see but in the things you cannot.

Oh, how you need to consider all the ways God has protected you that you've never seen. You didn't experience the drunk driver who never crashed into your minivan because God protected you, turning the car away from the intersection where your family was heading. You didn't die from a viral infection because God protected you, keeping you from touching a virus-contaminated door handle when a person walking out the same door held it open just as you arrived. A family emergency kept you from making a run to the store where a gunman would have robbed and shot you. For personal reasons you decided not to take the job where the boss would have mistreated and fired you after a few months.

Every day we are living in a world of narrow misses that we will never know about. Peter experienced the flogging. He had no experience of the deliberations that might have ended his life. Sometimes God is protecting you the most when you are able to see it the least.

GOD'S LOVE PROTECTS YOU FROM YOUR ENEMIES

Of all the bad things in life, enemies are my least favorite. Throughout my life, I've been ill, I've been injured, and I've been opposed. Being opposed is the worst. The terrible thing about having enemies is the presence of ill intent. This is what separates the opposition of enemies from the general kinds of trouble we just looked at. As terrible as trouble is, that pain comes without intent. Enemies, however, create much of the same damage and pain that other forms of trouble create with the added pain of their desire to destroy. Enemies take the presence of pain and make it personal. This is horrifying and debilitating for many of us.

The appalling reality of enemies is one we all must face sooner or later. Those enemies could be bullies in the playground, ruthless associates at your place of business, cruel neighbors, or even a pastor, spouse, child, or parent. Enemies come in all shapes, sizes, and seasons of life. Not all these enemies are created equal, but some are very influential and powerful, possessing the ability to change your life or destroy it.

In a world full of powerful people who hate us and seek to destroy us, we need a strong protector who loves us. That is just what God is for his people. The Bible makes clear that God's protection is part of his love: "My God in his steadfast love will meet me; God will let me look in triumph on my enemies" (Psalm 59:10). In fact, God's love provides strong confidence against every enemy you will ever face in your entire life: "In your steadfast love you will cut off my enemies, and you will destroy all the adversaries of my soul" (Psalm 143:12). Because of this glorious display of love, God's people have great confidence to cry out for his help in the face of every enemy:

> Attend to my cry,
> > for I am brought very low!
> Deliver me from my persecutors,
> > for they are too strong for me! (Psalm 142:6)

Even a man as famous and faithful as Peter had enemies. Peter's enemies were men who punished him with prison and with beatings for his faithfulness as a servant of Jesus. I explained earlier that these punishments were horrible and might have been fatal. Perhaps the worst thing was that Peter's enemies were religious leaders. I know many broken people have enemies like this.

Has a religious leader ever been one of your enemies? One of the most painful relationships I have ever had was with an older man in ministry that I once greatly respected and still deeply love. He befriended me, betrayed me, repeatedly tried to harm me, and to this day refuses to be reconciled with me.

I know my experience may not compare to what you have endured. But it is always tragic when ministers who are called to represent the great God of love behave in ways that are hateful and cruel. God can protect you from sinister enemies even when they call themselves his servants. Peter experienced ruthless treatment from religious leaders but still spoke of himself and all of God's people as those "who by God's power are being guarded through faith for a salvation ready to be revealed in the last time" (1 Peter 1:5). The damage Peter experienced from some of God's corrupt servants did not lead him to fail to trust the loving protection of God himself. You should not allow such treatment to derail your trust in God either.

As terrible as Peter's human enemies were, he faced another enemy that was far worse. Peter had spiritual enemies invisible to the naked eye that were far more dangerous than those he could see. One of the most sober declarations in all of Scripture comes to Peter when Jesus declares to him, "Satan demanded to have you, that he might sift you like wheat" (Luke 22:31). That bone-chilling statement reveals the existence of a dark and sinister enemy who seeks the destruction of a follower of Jesus. Satan desires to do to Peter's life what one would do to a handful of wheat as it is pressed through a sieve. But Jesus does not let Peter linger in fear over this powerful enemy. In the same breath that he gives the warning, Jesus promises protection: "But I have prayed for you that your faith may not fail" (Luke 22:32). Even though Satan demands Peter, Jesus refuses to give up his servant, instead covering his life in the loving and powerful prayers of God the Son protecting Peter from ultimate danger.

Unfortunately, the spiritual enemy of Peter is your enemy as well. Peter warns that "your adversary the devil prowls around like a roaring lion" (1 Peter 5:8). The devil is a real threat to your life. He threatens to destroy your marriage (1 Corinthians 7:5), your health (2 Corinthians 12:7), and your church (2 Timothy 2:26). As the enemy of humanity, he blinds people from believing in Jesus Christ (2 Corinthians 4:4).

Satan is the most powerful enemy you will ever face, but God loves you and has not given you over to him. God has delivered us from the dark domain of the devil through Jesus Christ, who defeated him on the cross (Colossians 1:13; 2:14–15). The devil is a powerful enemy, but God loves you more than Satan hates you, and God's ability to protect you is far greater than Satan's ability to destroy you (1 John 4:4).

GOD'S LOVE PROTECTS YOU
FROM YOURSELF

We have discussed the terror of trouble and the horror of human and spiritual enemies, but we still have not discussed your greatest enemy. The most significant threat to your life *is you*. The trouble of hurricanes, the pain of hateful people, and even the raging of the devil have nothing on your hard and sinful heart. The greatest threat to your life, happiness, and eternal joy is that, down deep in your heart, you love things God hates and hate things God loves. You are a sinner. And that reality has devastating consequences.

Think about the gifts that God gives to you, which we examined in the last chapter. Your sin threatens each one of those things. We endanger God's gift of life through a range of sinful behavior from drunkenness to gluttony. We endanger God's loving grant of a good reputation through shameful sins of gossip, lying, hypocrisy, and more. We endanger God's financial provision through sins of greed, stealing, and reckless spending. Most crucially, all our sin—the ones everyone sees and the ones no one sees—separates us from the God of great love:

> They will cry to the LORD,
>> but he will not answer them;
> he will hide his face from them at that time,
>> because they have made their deeds evil.
>> (Micah 3:4)

Your greatest enemy is yourself. But your loving father in heaven knows how to protect you even from yourself. God protects you from subtle sins, "Declare me innocent from hidden faults," and against high-handed sins, "Keep back your servant also from presumptuous sins; let them not have dominion over me!" (Psalm 19:12–13). God protects you from the stupid sins you committed a long time ago: "Remember not the sins of my youth or my transgressions; according to your steadfast love remember me" (Psalm 25:7). There is no sin you can commit that God will not protect you from in his love:

> In love you have delivered my life
>> from the pit of destruction,
> for you have cast all my sins
>> behind your back. (Isaiah 38:17)

Even though he was a famous and influential leader in the church and even though he faced dark and deadly enemies, Peter's worst enemy was himself. A significant portion of Peter's fame was that he was a complete wreck. He spoke up too soon, too loudly, and too often. In one of his most famous acts, he rebuked Jesus—the Son of God!—for wanting to go to Jerusalem to die for his people (Matthew 16:22). In another famous act, Peter denied his affiliation with Jesus, not once, and not twice, but three times (Luke 22:54–62). Later in his life, Peter needed to be rebuked by Paul because his behavior was undermining the ministry of Jesus (Galatians 2:11–14).

The best thing to say about Peter is not that he was a good man but that he knew himself to be a bad man who believed in God's ability to protect him from himself. That is why he wrote of Jesus, "He himself bore our sins in his body on the tree, that we might die to sin and live to righteousness" (1 Peter 2:24). This is a message that Peter had applied to himself that he also wanted you to know as well. Jesus became a sacrifice to deliver you from your worst enemy, yourself.

GOD'S LOVE PROTECTS YOU FROM WRATH

Sin interrupts your pursuit of a happy life, but this is not the worst thing about it. The worst thing about your sin is that it arouses God's wrath. Wrath is God's hatred of sin and his commitment to punish it, which he expresses throughout the Bible. The Gospel of

John records, "Whoever believes in the Son has eternal life; whoever does not obey the Son shall not see life, but the wrath of God remains on him" (3:36). Romans 2:5 says, "Because of your hard and impenitent heart you are storing up wrath for yourself on the day of wrath when God's righteous judgment will be revealed." Paul warned, "Let no one deceive you with empty words, for because of these things the wrath of God comes upon the sons of disobedience" (Ephesians 5:6).

The sin of his creation kindles God's wrath. Because God is righteous, he cannot allow sin to go unpunished. The Bible promises, "He will by no means clear the guilty, visiting the iniquity of the fathers on the children, to the third and the fourth generation" (Numbers 14:18).

God's righteous character requires that he punish unrighteous behavior. I learned this from my Mammaw. You have a Mammaw too, but you probably call her Grandma or Nanna. My Mammaw, Opal Jones, was not perfect but came closer to it than anyone else I know. She started out as a babysitter my mom hired when she went back to work a few weeks after I was born. Mammaw babysat me, my twin brother, and her own grandchildren.

We called her Mammaw because that's what her grandkids called her. Eventually we just became part of her family, she stopped taking money for watching us, and the line between us and her real grandkids evaporated. That line was never more invisible than when we got in trouble. When our rabble of kids were at Mammaw's house, we did our best to get into mischief, but we had to do it quietly. We didn't want Mammaw to know, and when she found out—and she found out a lot—we were in big trouble.

Mammaw's displeasure over our disobedience was always unpleasant. The sorrow of disappointing her often came with physical pain as well. Mammaw punished us when we disobeyed because she was a good and righteous woman. It would have been a mark against her character to encounter our disobedience and act like it didn't matter.

God is like this. Yet unlike my Mammaw, he is perfectly righteous and all knowing. There is no way for people to conceal their sin and no way for him to look the other way when we sin. God must punish sin because God is righteous.

This also means wrath is a different kind of divine attribute than love. Wrath flows from God's righteousness in response to human sinfulness. But love flows directly from the heart of God. God *has* wrath, but God *is* love.

The glorious good news is that God's great love has found a way to overrule our sin and protect us from wrath. When I was talking about how God must punish sin, I pointed to Numbers 14:18, *He will by no means clear the guilty*. But that is only a portion of that passage. I left off the first part: "The LORD is slow to anger and abounding in steadfast love, forgiving iniquity and transgression, but he will by no means clear the guilty." In this passage, God's anger is minimized in contrast to his love, which is maximized.

God is slow to anger, but he is abounding in steadfast love. The way he proves that is by responding to iniquity and transgression with forgiveness instead of wrath. This is a remarkable insight into the heart of God. God, in his great love, desires to withhold his wrath and lavish his love upon sinful people.

How can this be true? There is an undeniable tension between the two parts of this verse. In the first part of the passage, the Bible says that God is slow to anger, abounding in love, and forgiving sin. In the second part of the passage, the Bible says that he will by no means clear the guilty. So how can God bridge the gap between his love and forgiveness on one side and his anger and punishment on the other?

Peter felt the weight of that question. He knew the sinful mess of his life, and he knew he deserved punishment for the things he had done. But Peter also found the answer to that question in all that Jesus Christ came to be and do.

Peter knew that Jesus Christ came to earth as the sinless Son of God. Peter knew that when Jesus was punished on the cross, that punishment was not for Jesus's sins but for ours. Peter knew that Jesus was the bridge between God's love and God's wrath. Jesus satisfied God's wrath so that we could experience God's love and forgiveness. That is why Peter said, "For Christ also suffered once for sins, the righteous for the unrighteous, that he might bring us to God" (1 Peter 3:18).

God's love protects his people. In his love, God protects you from trouble. If you wonder how that can be true because of all the trouble you see, then think about all the trouble you do not see that God has spared you from without your knowledge.

God has loved you, protecting you from your physical and spiritual enemies. God has protected you from your sin. And, more than anything else, he has protected you from the punishment your sin deserves through the love of Jesus, who ultimately protects us from God's wrath (1 Thessalonians 1:10).

CHAPTER 7

God Loves You Even When Life Hurts

When I thought, "My foot slips,"
your steadfast love, O LORD, held me up.

PSALM 94:18

The sun was bright and shiny on a wondrously beautiful day. It seemed impossible that any pain could disrupt the splendor. Kids were running, adults were laughing, birds were singing, and palm trees were swaying in the balmy Florida breeze. My neighbor's yard was jammed with kids and sprinkled with adults. I was standing amid a crush of activity when my daughter came skipping—literally, skipping—around the corner of the house. The moment our eyes met, a wide smile opened on her face, and she started running toward me.

She was moving quickly with a bright face, but my face was twisted and angry. I opened my eyes wide with fury and screamed in a harsh and scary voice, "CHLOE, STOP! TURN AROUND! GO AWAY!"

She stopped, suddenly exchanging her bright smile for shocked fear. Apprehensive, she started to move toward me again, when, in an act of angry repetition, I shouted, "I MEAN IT! GO AWAY!"

I was not kidding, and she knew it. Tears filled her eyes as she obeyed, turned around, and walked away in painful and confused rejection.

Many of us feel about God's love the way my daughter felt about me that day in the yard. We are confused. We encounter God's love, we long for it, we yearn to experience God's loving embrace. Then just as we are running into God's compassionate arms, we feel tossed to the ground and rejected.

This experience of rejection is what we feel whenever we doubt God's love for us. These painful experiences of doubt can morph into objections to the great love of God. If God is love, then why don't I feel loved? If God were really loving, why is this bad thing happening? Every objection to God's love is based on personal doubt about that love.

Many people doubt God's love. A world as full of pain as this one generates buckets of objections to the great love of God. Some wonder how it is possible that God can behave so ruthlessly in the Old Testament, like when he commands his people to attack their enemies and let nothing that breathes remain alive (Deuteronomy 20:16). How can the God whose existence defines love give such a brutal command?

Others wonder about doctrines in the Bible that seem to teach that God chooses only some for salvation. Every person who trusts the Bible must struggle with how it is possible that all the verses in the Bible about God's love can be true and all the verses in the Bible about the doctrine of election can also be true. The two don't seem to go together.

There are answers to these and other objections, but it isn't necessary to deal with each one. The common thread uniting every objection to the love of God is that some people seem to experience more of the love of God than others. So, I'm going to address that common thread by dealing with two of the most significant objections people have that lead them to doubt the love of God.

If I can show that God's love endures in the face of these significant objections, it will provide a guide for responding to other objections. The first objection we'll consider is the reality of suffering. If God loves me, why does he allow me to suffer?

TOUGH LOVE?

If God protects his people, then why do those he loves and promises to protect experience so much pain? That is *the* question, isn't it?

Let me ask it more starkly. If God is the very definition of love, the one who delights in his people, lavishes them with wonderful gifts, and protects them from danger, then how is it possible that the very people who are objects of God's love can experience such crushing suffering?

It is impossible to write a book on God's love without dealing with this issue honestly and candidly. If you know God, you are aware of the remarkable gifts that he has given to you, and you know some of the protections that he has extended to defend you from danger. As wonderful as those things are, you also have experienced soul-strangling suffering. Even though you were faithful and begged God for rescue, your spouse still walked out on you, you lost your life savings, your friend quit speaking to you, your baby died, your cancer came back, or some other terrible tragedy has befallen you. If God loves you, then why does he allow so much pain?

ASKING "WHY?"

This was the question asked by Martha and Mary when their brother Lazarus died. These three siblings spent significant time near Jesus during his time on earth. They knew him, loved him, and he loved them: "Now Jesus loved Martha and her sister and Lazarus" (John 11:5).

But Lazarus got very sick. We have no idea what his affliction was. The only indication we have of the sickness is a statement that tells us more about Jesus's love than Lazarus's illness: "Lord, he whom you love is ill" (John 11:3). Whatever the illness was, it was serious because it ultimately took Lazarus's life. In fact, by the time Jesus got to his friend, Lazarus had already been dead four days (John 11:17).

Consider this excruciating experience of death for a moment. The death of a loved one is an incredibly painful process. If you have never experienced this, it is one of the hardest parts of life, and none of us can escape it. I sat at the bedside of my mother in the weeks leading up to her death. Watching the life slowly escape from the body of someone you love is utterly tormenting. The pressure of doing everything possible to extend life, of trying to communicate last words, express love, and ensure comfort, all while managing the rest of your life, which keeps on going, feels like an impossible task.

Mary and Martha went through every painful second of this.

Their experience doesn't consider the depth of Lazarus's suffering as he slowly grew sicker, as he experienced the dawning realization that he might not get better, as he dealt with inevitable doubts and questions about what was waiting for him in eternity after his eyes closed in death. It doesn't consider his weakness, his fear, or his pain as death wrapped its merciless clutches around his life, forcing it out to the last gasp.

Then there was the grief awaiting Martha and Mary after their final goodbyes when Lazarus's life finally slipped away. There was the ache in the heart, the pressure in the stomach, the uncontrollable sobbing as they experienced wave upon wave of realization that they would never again see their brother. They experienced all the painful volley of emotions as they laughed at a delightful memory of Lazarus only to weep at the realization that they would never experience such moments again. Grief is ghastly. And Martha and Mary went through four punishing days of it.

Martha and Mary occupied no privileged perch of pious spirituality. They struggled through their grief the same way you and I do. They struggled with questions. One question was particularly pressing. When Jesus finally arrived after Lazarus was dead and buried, the first thing Martha said to him was, "Lord, if you had been here, my brother would not have died" (John 11:21). Mary said the exact same thing: "Lord, if you had been here, my brother would not have died" (John 11:32).

Those might look like statements, but I promise, they are questions. Massive questions marks hover over each assertion. *Why?* pierces through each identical statement. The reason Martha and Mary made the exact same point with identical words is because they had been talking. In the long days that stretched between asking

Jesus for help and when he finally showed up, they spent hours thinking, wondering, praying, and discussing, "Where is Jesus? We know he *can* help. We know he *wants* to help. Where is he?"

Jesus was a no-show, and the people who needed him wondered why.

Martha and Mary weren't the only ones asking questions. Jesus's enemies were also wondering. Many of the religious leaders of the day were threatened by the popularity of Jesus and the attention he was stealing from them. They wanted to put an end to his ministry. Those enemies saw Jesus arrive so long after the funeral. They witnessed all the pain that had been caused by the death of Lazarus, they reflected on Jesus's incredible power, and they scoffed, "Could not he who opened the eyes of the blind man also have kept this man from dying?" (John 11:37).

There is an important lesson in this for us as we ask our own questions of God during pain and loss. In the throes of suffering, it is possible to ask the same question from two very different perspectives. Martha and Mary knew Jesus. They loved him, they wanted to trust him, but they could not understand why Jesus acted as he did. In their struggle, they went to their friend and asked him why.

Jesus's enemies were likewise confused. In their struggle, they asked their enemy why. Jesus's friends ask why from the standpoint of trust and humility. Jesus's enemies ask why from the standpoint of anger and mockery.

No one is rebuked for asking questions. The concern in the Scripture is the spirit behind the question. It is right for God's people to bring him all their cares, concerns, and questions. The lesson we learn from Martha and Mary is to ask our questions as friends, not enemies.

WHEN LOVE DELAYS

In pain and suffering, Jesus is a friend with friendly intentions. This is as true for you right now as it was true for Martha, Mary, and Lazarus. Jesus loved this trio of siblings, and he delayed in going to Lazarus's side. Even though Jesus's love seems at odds with his delay, the Bible connects his love and his delay in a shocking way. The Bible says Jesus's love *caused* his delay: "Now Jesus loved Martha and her sister and Lazarus. So, when he heard that Lazarus was ill, he stayed two days longer in the place where he was" (John 11:5–6).

Jesus's response is surprising to us. It seems shockingly out of place. Delaying the way Jesus did does not seem like a loving thing to do. It is certainly not what I did the day my father died. That day is seared in my mind.

He collapsed at work and was rushed to the hospital by paramedics, who reported he was unresponsive. I heard the news when my brother called my office to tell me Dad was being taken to the hospital. I hung up the phone, stood to my feet, and drove immediately to the hospital. I went to the hospital right away because I love my dad, and I knew love required urgency. Jesus's response stuns us when we look at his response through the lens of love requiring urgency.

But love does not always require urgency. Sometimes love requires delay. A few years ago, my son was experiencing cruelty and mistreatment from some students at school. Anyone who has experienced such harshness knows how painful those situations can be, and my son was in turmoil over it.

One day he pled with me not to make him go back to school. I turned to him, put my hands on his shoulders, and told him that I loved him with all my heart, but that there was no way in the world I was going to allow him to quit going to school. When he heard this response from me, he fell onto my shoulder sobbing. He begged me to reconsider.

I did not. My heart broke for my precious son. We worked together on strategies to respond well to people who were mistreating him, and he ultimately changed schools at the end of the academic year, but he remained in school.

I responded to my dad with urgency, and I responded to my son with delay. The responses were opposite but shared the same motivation. My love for my dad led me to respond with urgency, and my love for my son led me to respond with delay. Delay demonstrates love just as much as urgency. The difference depends on the knowledge of the person showing love. With my dad, I knew I needed to get to him quickly. With my son, I knew he needed to be patient, to be faithful in hardship, and to learn lessons he never would have if I had removed him from the painful situation.

The reality of life in a fallen world is that there are times when it is good for us to endure pain and bad for us to avoid it. You and I make decisions every day to place ourselves in difficult situations because we believe it is better to endure the difficulty than to avoid it. My most significant decision like this was the choice to have brain surgery.

For years I had been treating spasms on the right side of my body with nonsurgical interventions, which were not working. Finally, my wife and I sat across from my neurosurgeon, who explained that the only way I could fully resolve the problem was with surgery on my brain. That surgery was the most challenging physical experience I had ever endured. It involved drilling a hole in the base of my skull and manipulating the nerves in my brain.

When the surgery was over, they sealed up the back of my head with bone putty and dozens of stitches. During the monthlong recovery, I dealt with incomprehensible pain, difficulty walking, inability to use the bathroom alone, disorientation, sleeplessness, nausea, dizziness. Even more, before they could even remove my stitches, I caught a nasty case of COVID-19.

Then, after eight months, I made the decision to go through the entire ordeal again when they discovered they needed to make revisions on the first surgery. I made the decision to endure months of pain and difficulty because I knew the path to long-term joy was the path through short-term pain.

In fact, I discovered while completing this book that neither surgery worked to resolve my neurological difficulties. A mistake in the second surgery actually made things far worse. Eventually a different set of doctors at a completely different hospital had to do a third surgery to fix the problem and relieve the pressure on my nerve. The third attempt appears to have worked, but repeated surgeries compromised the tissue around my brain, leading to a leak of spinal fluid that required a fourth brain surgery to correct. This incredible season was the most physically difficult of my life—utterly dwarfing the pain and difficulty of the first two surgeries. Agonizing pain, unmanageable dizziness, and isolation from family and friends for weeks in an intensive care unit often felt overwhelming.

Even though I experienced painful and years-long delays in my recovery, my confidence in God's love for me grew rather than diminished. I trust God was loving me with delay. If I can trust myself and medical doctors to make decisions to endure short-term pain for the potential of long-term gain, then I can trust God to send me through difficulty he desires with the guarantee of eternal gain. You, too, can trust God with your delay.

God is characterized by perfect love and wisdom, so when we see that Jesus loved Lazarus with delay, we do not need to wonder at it. Instead, we should be excited about the good thing he is going to do to show his love and power through Lazarus's suffering. That excitement will pay off as we see that the good thing Jesus had in mind for Lazarus and his family was wonderful beyond anything this grieving family could have dreamt.

While the family was enduring a loving delay, Jesus walked through the grieving and scoffing crowd and did something else nobody understood—he asked them to remove the stone covering Lazarus's tomb. Martha responded cautiously to this supreme oddity, "Lord, by this time there will be an odor, for he has been dead four days" (John 11:39).

Here is another question masquerading as a statement. Martha cannot understand why Jesus, having arrived too late to help Lazarus before he died, is now going to make his family endure the stink of his decaying remains.

Jesus proceeded undeterred. As the stone was taken away, the stench of death flooded the nostrils of the confused crowd. Jesus, confounding the crowd even more, stared into the black tomb and yelled at the top of his lungs, "Lazarus, come out" (John 11:43).

We must pause here. This really is the low point. If you know this story, your familiarity with it might keep you from experiencing this moment the way the original audience did. Jesus, just dripping with tardiness, stands among a grieving family and gives orders to open the grave. Overwhelming them with the fresh smell of a rotting corpse, he screams into the tomb that the dead man should do something that dead men don't do and come out of the tomb.

The behavior looks cruel, insensitive, untimely, inexplicable, even insane. And that is how the crowd would have received it. You can see in your mind the sideways glances. You can hear the crowd murmuring that the guy had lost it. You can understand they were thinking he was a madman. It made sense for them to think that way.

But only for a moment.

Seconds after Jesus cried out his astonishing command, death bowed in submission to its Lord and Master and broke its hold on the one it had engulfed in its clutches. In spite of themselves, Lazarus's dead ears heard the voice of their Lord and King. Lazarus's lifeless corpse obeyed the master of the universe and rose from the slab, despite the instincts of every dead body in history. The tragedy was reversed. Lazarus walked out of the tomb.

Can you imagine the gasps, the screams, the shocked looks, the dropped jaws? Can your mind envision the overwhelming wonder as the smell of death vanished and a living Lazarus filled their gaze? Some would have fainted from the shock. Others would have dropped to their knees, overcome by the glorious display of power and love.

I imagine Martha and Mary running to their brother and embracing him. I'm sure the three siblings quickly found their way to Jesus as he surrounded them in an embrace of perfect love.

This astonishing moment was the one Jesus had in mind when his love delayed. It was this moment of joy and glory he was planning the entire time. Jesus's plan was so much better than what the family desired. They could not see it, but Jesus knew he was going to do more than reverse an illness. He was going to reverse the irreversible. Jesus was going to do the absolutely impossible. He was going to reverse death.

He knew that when he did, the family would be completely overwhelmed with joy and wonder. That night there would have been stunned silence as they sat staring at each other, enjoying moments they were certain they would never enjoy again.

Years later, they would still be tossing their heads back in laughter and astonishment that Lazarus's life had been restored after it ended. For the rest of their lives, they would have told the story of the overwhelming display of love and glory that they experienced in their hour of deepest darkness.

A HIGHER PURPOSE

When Jesus's love was delayed, he had more in mind than just that moment of physical resurrection. Everything about Jesus's engagement with the grieving family indicates he had something greater in mind than bringing a dead man back to life. One of Jesus's responses to the grieving sisters when he arrived was a glorious promise: "I am the resurrection and the life. Whoever believes in me, though he die, yet shall he live, and everyone who lives and believes in me shall never die. Do you believe this?" (John 11:25–26).

In front of the staring crowd at Lazarus's tomb, Jesus prayed, "Father, I thank you that you have heard me. I knew that you always hear me, but I said this on account of the people standing around, that they may believe that you sent me." (John 11:41–42). Jesus's goal went beyond reversing the effects of death one time in one man for one family. Jesus came to be the source of resurrection life for anyone who would trust in him across the entire globe and throughout all of history. This one miracle would prove his power to grant eternal life to anyone who would believe at any time and in any place. The glorious reversal of suffering in the life of Lazarus, Martha, and Mary was a grand demonstration of who he is so that soon the entire world would see.

This fact was remarkably good news for Lazarus and his family.

Yet, no matter how delighted the sisters would be to have their brother back, regardless of Lazarus's joy in being restored to life, and despite all the family joys that would have been experienced after Lazarus's return to life—it was all temporary. Lazarus was alive, but at some painful point in the future, Lazarus died again. People he loved had to say goodbye to him again. He had to suffer again. He had to face the final enemy again.

Jesus's miracle was amazing, but it couldn't make Lazarus happy forever. The best news about the miracle is that it proved—beyond any doubt—that Jesus is who he says he is and that he is able to provide eternal life beyond any grave to all who trust in him—*everyone who lives and believes in me shall never die.*

Jesus's plan to love his friends with delay and pain was harder than they would have chosen but was better for them than they could have imagined. Lazarus, Martha, and Mary are alive in heaven today—as promised—and are today unspeakably grateful for Jesus's loving delay. In that loving lack of urgency, he accomplished so much of eternal good.

He taught each of them not just how to live a little longer but how to live forever by trusting him. He accomplished great glory as an entire crowd of people were convinced that Jesus was in fact the great God of heaven and earth come in the flesh. When they each faced their own deaths after this event, they would have done it with more hope and grace as they trusted in Jesus's promise of eternal life when their eyes closed in death.

These siblings have now lived in heaven with Christ for over 2,000 years and have seen their story used millions of times throughout history to encourage others in pain, to grant faith, to strengthen hope, and to change lives as their story of pain leads to grace for more and more people. It happens to people every time the glory of Jesus is recounted in their story of pain. It is happening to you right now.

The pain was excruciating, but it was worth it. What was true for them is also true for you. My friend, I could wish that it weren't so, but suffering is coming for you. It is worse than that. Since you're reading this, you have not yet experienced the ultimate suffering that awaits you at the end of life as you face your own death. Unfortunately, between that future moment and this current one, there are countless trials and sufferings that await you. You can't know the content of all that pain, but it will be terrible. You will ache in your body and soul more than you can fathom right now, and you will cry countless tears.

As hard as it will all be, I want to make you a promise. It's a promise that comes from the pages of Scripture with the full authority of God, whose great love has cared for you every day of your life in every instance of pain. The promise comes from Jesus Christ, who promised with his own mouth that *everyone who lives and believes in me shall never die.* Here is the promise: your losses will never last. They will always give way to infinite gain.

Every loss you ever experience will be something temporary that you can't keep anyway. The loving purpose of God is for you to lose nothing that is ultimate or eternal. The God who loves you by giving you wonderful things wants to love you with suffering. This is how the apostle James explains it: "Count it all joy, my brothers, when you meet trials of various kinds, for you know that the testing of your faith produces steadfastness. And let steadfastness have its full effect, that you may be perfect and complete, lacking in nothing" (James 1:2–4).

We often think of suffering in terms of what we lose. But the Bible speaks of suffering in terms of what we gain. The God of great love says the purpose of pain is that we would be *perfect and complete, lacking in nothing.* From the divine perspective, suffering is a gift. It is an expression of love. God uses suffering so that when it is over, we have *more*—never less.

The apostle Peter explains how suffering can be gain and loss can be a gift. "Now for a little while, if necessary, you have been grieved by various trials, so that the tested genuineness of your faith—more precious than gold that perishes though it is tested by fire—may be found to result in praise and glory and honor at the revelation of Jesus Christ" (1 Peter 1:6–7).

Suffering tests the genuineness of our faith. Because God loves us, he is always bestowing his wonderful gifts. As we receive these gifts, it is crucial to be sure we love the giver not the gifts. Jesus's promise of life beyond the grave doesn't come to those who trust God's gifts but to those who trust in him. In a world where everything we have is the gift of a loving giver, there is only one way to know whether we love and trust God or the gifts God gives. That one way is for God to take some of his gifts away. When he takes away his gifts and we curse him, we know it was never him that we loved. But when God takes away his good gifts and we still love him, we know our faith is genuine and that we have life with him forever.

God sometimes takes away his temporal gifts through suffering in order to ensure we receive his eternal gifts by really trusting him. Even in suffering—especially in suffering—God is loving you. God is delighting in you. God is giving you wonderful things. He is protecting you from an eternity apart from him. As the apostle Paul says, "For this light momentary affliction is preparing for us an eternal weight of glory beyond all comparison, as we look not to the things that are seen but to the things that are unseen. For the things that are seen are transient, but the things that are unseen are eternal" (2 Corinthians 4:17–18).

Our temporary hardships on earth are preparing us for eternal happiness in heaven. We know God is loving us and giving us wonderful things even in our worst moments. God's love uses delay, pain, and loss to deliver us from what can never last to grant what we can never lose.

Do you remember how I began this chapter with a story about my daughter? That day, as she ran toward me in my neighbor's yard, I made her cry with a stern rebuke and a face filled with anger and urgency. She was running at me with great joy in the full expectation that I would receive her in my loving embrace. Instead, I screamed loudly and aggressively for her to go away. Her heart was broken by my harshness. As you read my account, you were probably concerned as well. Why would a loving father behave with such cruelty?

What Chloe did not see and what I did not share with you is that there was a very large water moccasin jumping and hissing in the grass between me and my daughter. This deadly poisonous snake had only one path of escape—directly toward my daughter! With no time to explain and knowing she might not recognize the danger of this vicious snake, I shouted at her to go away. Seconds after she cleared the scene, my friend tossed me a shovel, which I used to attack and kill the snake.

I knew what she did not—that if my daughter had come even a few feet closer, she could have been bitten and killed. My harsh behavior that day was motivated by love, even though my little girl could not immediately see it. Once she understood, she was grateful for the tough love I had shown her in that moment. God loves us this way more than we know, and if we only understood all that he did on our behalf and for our good, we would never question his heart of love for us.

GOD SUFFERS TOO

Jesus's plan for his friends included more pain for them than they probably wanted. But they were not the only ones who suffered. God himself endured the pain as well. As Jesus witnessed the loss of his friend and the grief of his close friends, he endured grief too: "He was deeply moved in his spirit and greatly troubled" (John 11:33). Later, his profound emotion is revealed in the simple statement, "Jesus wept" (John 11:35). Jesus was in such pain that he broke down and sobbed.

This is an incredible piece of the story. Don't rush past this detail. Remember that it was Jesus who made a decision to love his friends with delay and pain. Remember that it was Jesus who, as he stood at the tomb, was aware of the explosive power he was about to unleash in undoing death. Jesus knew what he was doing. But when the hearts of Jesus's friends broke, his broke too. When the people Jesus loved cried, he cried with them. The sovereignty of God joins up with the love of God to create divine sympathy in our pain. God is always accomplishing his purposes in our pain but never in a way characterized by cold calculation. God's most difficult work is always done with gentleness, sensitivity, and care.

Jesus's suffering is not limited to his sympathy for people going through hard times. Jesus went through more suffering than anyone in human history. Jesus knew what it was to be wrongly accused, tried, and convicted. Jesus experienced torture as a crown of thorns was pressed upon his skull, as he felt the strike of the lash repeatedly across his precious back, and as nails and spears were thrust into his perfect body while he hung suffocating and bleeding on a rough cross. He felt the full weight of divine wrath as he was punished for sins he never committed.

Jesus's suffering and death was horrendous and terrible. He suffered more than you or I ever will. He experienced greater loss than we can fathom. And his suffering gives meaning and purpose to our suffering. "But we see him who for a little while was made lower than the angels, namely Jesus, crowned with glory and honor because of the suffering of death, so that by the grace of God he might taste death for everyone" (Hebrews 2:9).

Jesus tasted death for everyone. That includes you. He is now crowned with glory and honor precisely because of his tremendous suffering. God's delay when Jesus was on the cross was a display of love to his Son and is a display of love to you. With that delay, God took the most horrible instance of human suffering and turned it around for honor, glory, and everlasting good.

Throughout endless ages, all who trust in Jesus will look at his horrible suffering as fuel for their eternal praise of who he is and what he did for them. The great love and power of God combine to turn the worst instance of suffering into the greatest demonstration of good in the history of humanity. If God's great love can turn the worst suffering for good, then he can turn yours for good too. You watch. Trust the one who gives life beyond the grave and then wait and see. It will be better than you can possibly imagine.

CHAPTER 8

The Great Love of God and the Existence of Hell

Has God forgotten to be gracious?
Has he in anger shut up his compassion?
PSALM 77:9

The same Bible that shouts the magnificent glories of the love of God also proclaims the shocking horrors of hell. Jesus talks about hell as much as any other person in the Bible and describes it as the destination for all those who do not follow him (Mark 9:43). In that place they will join the devil and his demons (Matthew 25:41). He describes it as a fiery place of torture where people only cry and grind their teeth in pain (Matthew 13:50). There is no end to this punishment which endures forever (Jude 1:7). In one of the most horrifying descriptions I have ever encountered, Jesus describes hell as the place "where their worm does not die and the fire is not quenched" (Mark 9:48). The horror in this description is found in the fact that the bodies of the people in hell provide fuel for the fire and the food for the worms. The fire never goes out because its fuel is never consumed. The worm never dies because forever and ever its food remains. This is a description of the eternal existence of people in hell that is as graphic and terrible as anything you could imagine.

That description comes from the lips of Jesus Christ, the author of life and the very embodiment of love. Do you remember John, the apostle of love who learned that God is love from spending time with Jesus? While he was with Jesus, he would have heard Jesus make these shocking statements about hell. Even though John heard these statements with his own ears, they did not compromise his belief in God's great love. John continued to believe in the great love of God when he heard teaching on hell, and you can too. This chapter explains how that is possible.

The Bible is full of teaching about hell, but there is only one place where we see a personal experience of what hell is actually like. In Luke 16, Jesus shares a parable about an unidentified man who went to hell. The parable does not tell us everything we need to know about hell, but there is much for us to learn from what happens to the man Jesus describes. For example, the experience of this anonymous man confirms that hell is a final destination, and those who go there are not permitted to leave (Luke 16:26). Hell is an eternal place of torment (Luke 16:23, 28) and anguish (16:24–25).

Yet, the words of Jesus clarify that the horrors of hell do not compromise the loving character of God. I want you to cherish four reasons why the existence of hell does not threaten the great love of God.

GOD'S LOVE IS A RIGHTEOUS LOVE

The Bible is clear about the kind of love God has. God's love is so wonderful because it is defined by perfect righteousness and faithfulness. God's eternal love delights, gives, and protects, and it is defined by moral perfection. God's love completely rejects sin and unrighteousness. "Righteousness and justice are the foundation of your throne; steadfast love and faithfulness go before you" (Psalm 89:14).

A tension exists between God's righteousness and love when we consider how God responds to sinful human beings. On the one hand, God loves all people and does not desire to mete out the terrible punishment of hell. "As I live, declares the Lord GOD, I have no pleasure in the death of the wicked, but that the wicked turn from his way and live; turn back, turn back from your evil ways, for why will you die?" (Ezekiel 33:11). The apostle Paul says that God "desires all people to be saved and to come to the knowledge of the truth" (1 Timothy 2:4).

In passages like these, God expresses a desire to avoid punishing people. Notice that God makes an earnest appeal to turn from sin, receive salvation, and avoid eternal punishment. Notice also that God never includes an option to avoid eternal punishment without turning from sin. It is true that God does not desire anyone to die, but it is also true that God does not desire to grant anyone eternal life without repentance. This is because God's love is characterized by righteousness.

God's love is so defined by righteousness that if he were to stop being righteous, then he would stop being the God of great love. That can never happen. For God to preserve his love, he must preserve his righteousness, and that means he cannot tolerate unrighteousness.

It helps me better understand this reality when I think about my own relationship with my children. When I tell you that I love them with all my heart, it is the honest truth. My personal goal is to never let a day go by without telling them that I love them and without showing my love in some way.

Because I love my children so much, I hate to punish them. I could say even more strongly that I have no desire to punish my children. But when my children disobey, it creates a tension in my response toward them. On the one hand, I want to love them without any punishment. On the other hand, I know I cannot allow their disobedience to go unaddressed and make me an accomplice to their sin.

If I don't punish them, they will grow up reckless and irresponsible. They will disrespect me, and our home will become a very unpleasant place where everyone lives selfishly. I cannot allow that to happen—*it would not be loving to them*. Even though I truly don't want to punish my children, I know defending righteousness requires punishment when my children disobey. That reality means that I choose to do what I otherwise would avoid and punish my children.

We can learn from this analogy, but there are places where it obviously fails. First, my kids and I are in the same situation before God. We are all sinners, and I am no more righteous than they are. Also my punishments, regardless of their severity, never come close to the terrible reality of a hell as a place of eternal punishment. Still another point of breakdown in the analogy is that I do not have an ability to give my children righteousness, but God is able to grant his righteousness to anyone who has faith in Jesus (Romans 3:23–34).

Our relationships with our children help us understand how it is possible to have love for another that strongly desires to avoid punishment while maintaining a fundamental commitment to punish sin in order to preserve righteousness. Our motives can be complex yet unified in what we ultimately seek and want. And this is even more true when we think of the perfect and holy heart of our loving God.

A lot of things are true about the nameless man whom Jesus talks about in Luke 16. He was a man of great wealth with many possessions and a big, gated home (Luke 16:19–20). The man lived a lavish lifestyle that included a great feast every day (Luke 16:19). He was also accustomed to giving orders and so was apparently a man with power (Luke 16:24). He was a man of incredible privilege.

What he did not have was righteousness. Of all the amazing things that were said of him, he lacked the one thing he most needed, righteousness, which would spare him from hell. The man's problem was not that God, who had lavished him with many gifts, had no heart of love for him—it was that the man had no heart for God.

Hell poses no problem for the love of God. The reason hell exists has less to do with the love of God and more to do with the sinfulness of people. Rightly understood, hell magnifies the great love of God. The God defined by perfect righteousness in his great love has enabled sinners to avoid the terrible punishment they deserve. God is not to blame when unrighteous people refuse to accept his loving provision to escape the punishment their sin deserves (Proverbs 5:21–23).

GOD'S LOVE IS A JEALOUS LOVE

God is not only defined by his righteousness—his commitment to always do what is right and just—but by jealousy. A crucial link exists between God's righteousness and his jealousy, which helps us better understand how God's love allows for the existence of hell. Throughout the Bible, God gives laws for his people to obey. The best summary of God's Old Testament Law is found in the Ten

Commandments. The first two commandments clarify that God is the only God, and it is right and good for him to have first place in every human heart:

> You shall have no other gods before me.
>
> You shall not make for yourself a carved image, or any likeness of anything that is in heaven above, or that is in the earth beneath, or that is in the water under the earth. (Exodus 20:3–4)

In these commands, God is reserving for himself exclusive status of honor and worship. God explains that his jealousy is the reason for these commands: "You shall not bow down to them or serve them, for I the LORD your God am a jealous God" (Exodus 20:5).

In the New Testament, when Jesus is asked about the greatest commandment in the entire Bible, he responds straightforwardly, "You shall love the Lord your God with all your heart and with all your soul and with all your mind" (Matthew 22:37). In each place, the language is different, but the principle is the same. Whether from Moses in the Old Testament or from Jesus in the New Testament, when you boil down the law, it is all about God being first in the hearts of his people.

The requirement to prioritize God is the reason we were created by God. It is the only right, just, and appropriate response of the human heart to our Creator. This is a problem because every human heart is now infected by the moral disease of sin. The essence of human sin is that we want ourselves, not God, to have the first position in our heart. We want to have that first position in the hearts of others as well. This is apparent in the very first sin ever committed.

When Satan tempted the first couple to eat the forbidden fruit, he knew how to gain a foothold in their hearts. He held out the perverse hope that they could achieve divinity, "God knows that when you eat of it your eyes will be opened, and you will be like God" (Genesis 3:5). Adam and Eve believed this lie, disobeyed, and plunged all humanity into the insane march to achieve a divine status we can never possess. Every sin we ever commit stems from jealously pursuing our own interests instead of God's, "Where jealousy and selfish ambition exist, there will be disorder and every vile practice" (James 3:16).

The essence of unrighteousness is humanity's pursuit of honor and exaltation that does not belong to us. God's commitment to uphold what is right and good, the worship that properly belongs only to him, gives rise to his jealousy. Yet God is not the only jealous one. Sinful people jealously desire what belongs only to God.

Now we begin to see the connection between God's righteousness and his jealousy. God deserves priority in every heart because he is God. The rules he gives as God are not onerous or unfair. They reflect the way things are intended to be for our ultimate happiness, where God has priority of status in every human heart.

Yet people do not respond to these rules with honor and respect for God, but with jealousy for their own name and fame. In our jealous pursuit of divinity, we deny God his rightful status, disobey his rules, and embrace unrighteousness. This unrighteousness arouses the jealous wrath of God, who demands first place in human hearts.

It is crucial that we understand *why* human jealousy is sinful and divine jealousy is righteous. Human jealousy is sinful because it desires a status we do not deserve and can never earn. God's jealousy is good—he is God and rightly deserves it. He is truly entitled to the first place in every heart, and God is committed to that place for our good and his glory. This requires God to be jealous.

If God stopped being jealous, he would break the first and greatest commandment, and he would fail to honor himself as the one true and living God. God would become a lawbreaker— thus unrighteous. For God to be unrighteous would mean he is no longer God. This will never happen.

All of human history reflects a struggle between God, who deserves to be first, and human beings, who want their supremacy. It is impossible for God to change and lose this conflict. The only way this war will end is for human beings to relinquish their corrupt claim on God's throne, but our sinful passion for priority has become part of the fabric of who we are. Our sinful self-exaltation has taken deep root in our heart.

The only hope is a miraculous intervention that changes our hearts and leads to repentance, our acknowledgment of God's claim to his throne and his rightful place of priority in every human heart, including our own. Peace comes when we relinquish our corrupt quest to be God and commit to placing him first, living according to his will instead of our own.

Repentance offers the only path through which we can avoid hell. Jesus said, "Unless you repent, you will all likewise perish" (Luke 13:5). No amount of judgment can make people turn from their sinful selfishness and desire to live life under the sovereign care of God. Even the horrible judgments in the last days before Jesus returns will not bring about the repentance of hard-hearted people.

When the book of Revelation describes the devastating bowls of God's wrath poured out on the sinful hordes of humanity alive in those days, their response is pure hard-heartedness: "People gnawed their tongues in anguish and cursed the God of heaven for their pain and sores. They did not repent of their deeds" (Revelation 16:10–11). Even when Jesus returns at the very end of time in glory and power, everyone will be forced to kneel and acknowledge the plain fact of Jesus's triumph, but without repentance there will be no change of heart and no joy in his victory (Philippians 2:10–11).

Repentance is also crucial because, without it, we don't want eternal life. Being a sinner means we are at war with God. Unrepentant sinners do not love God and do not desire him. Sin makes us jealous for our own glory in the face of the infinite God rightly jealous for his glory. Even if they do not state it, the actions and indifference of sinners really do show they hate God and do not want to be around him. They do not want to be in heaven.

This means that people who have broken hearts over their loved ones who won't repent, and the God who desires that none should perish, have a greater interest in rebels attaining eternal life than the rebels themselves. Rebels do not want what we want for them, and they do not desire God's free offer.

You see this in the resistance of the anonymous man in Jesus's parable in Luke 16. Though he is in the agony of hell, he refuses to stop the sinful self-obsession of living for his own glory. In the parable, Jesus portrays this tortured man as having the ability to look into heaven and see the great Abraham of old together with one of the beggars the unknown man knew while he was alive on earth.

When the tortured man stares out of hell into heaven, he puts himself first. He begins to bark out orders to Abraham and this former beggar. First, he wants the beggar now in heaven to come down to hell and cool his tongue with just a drop of water because he is desperate for relief (Luke 16:24). He even knows about repentance because he wants to warn his family who is still alive that they should repent, and so he orders Abraham to send the man to warn them (Luke 16:27–30).

This man is in eternal torment, and, as he sees into heaven, it occurs to him to insist someone come to serve his needs, and then to beg for someone to go to his family to encourage them to repent. It never occurs to him to want to be in heaven or to attempt repentance himself. In hell, he is willing to moan, complain, beg, and demand. He is not willing to repent.

My friend, as heartbreaking as it might be to think of eternal life without your loved ones, I promise you that heaven will not be enjoyable if it is full of rebels who are constantly disobeying God and disturbing the joy of the people who love him. These are people who don't *want* to be where God and his people are. Even more than that, a jealous God could never permit the sinful jealousy of human rebels—it would turn heaven into hell. And sadly, those rebels would never want heaven anyway.

GOD'S LOVE IS A PATIENT LOVE

When you think about the righteous jealousy of God and the sinful, selfish, unrighteousness of people, it brings out another element of God's great love. God's love is patient. For the length of your entire life and for the length of the life of everyone you know, you have been sinning against a righteous and jealous God. Every second you are not loving him with all your heart, soul, mind, and strength, you are falling short of the standard he has clearly laid out for you.

Every day you use gifts from his hand—your life, intellect, relationships, and speech—to spurn him and turn your back on him. God's love holds back an immediate display of his wrath. "The Lord is not slow to fulfill his promise as some count slowness, but is patient toward you, not wishing that any should perish, but that all should reach repentance" (2 Peter 3:9). Every day God is delaying judgment because of his loving and patient desire to see more people avoid the terrible fate of perishing in hell. God's patience is not passive but active.

God's patience actively warns about the dangers of hell for anyone who refuses to repent. He has sent many messengers to you and the ones you love, telling of the fiery judgment that waits for anyone who refuses to repent. These warnings demonstrate the compassion of the God of great love. These warnings come throughout life in various ways and at numerous times. This book is a warning. Jesus's parable of the perishing man in Luke 16 is a warning. Even the man in the parable was warned. It is clear in the parable that the man recognized the patriarch Abraham (16:24) and understood the need for repentance (16:30). Apparently, he did not take those messages to heart during his life. God extended patience to him, but he frittered it all away until he received the judgment he deserved. God's patience delays the punishment deserved for anyone who is alive today but has not trusted in Jesus. In a great act of love, he is delaying the punishment they deserve to keep them from perishing.

God's patience also leads people to himself in a more positive way than warnings. One way God extends his patient love is by lavishing people with the gifts of his love. We have already seen the mysterious man in Luke 16 received these gifts. All of God's gifts are meant to point people to the God of great love.

Paul says that God gives the gifts of life, breath, and a place to live so that people should "seek God, and perhaps feel their way toward him and find him" (Acts 17:27). Paul makes this same point even more clearly in the book of Romans: "What can be known about God is plain to them, because God has shown it to them. For his invisible attributes, namely, his eternal power and divine nature, have been clearly perceived, ever since the creation of the world, in the things that have been made. So they are without excuse" (Romans 1:19–20).

God's gifts point to God so clearly that God is known to everyone even if they have never read the Bible, heard a preacher, or had a conversation with a Christian friend. God is known so clearly through these gifts that point to him that all people are without excuse in the face of judgment.

It is impossible to see such patience and miss the greatness of God's love. God is righteous, and we are not. God is jealous for our affections, and we are jealous to keep them from him. We are his enemies, yet he responds to us with patient love. Every day of life he extends blessings and admonitions to rebellious people to woo and warn them from the fate they are pursuing. Hell is not a place for people who never experienced the love of God but a place for people who reject God's love day after day and year after year in spite of repeated warnings. Hell does not raise questions about God's love but underlines the sinful stubbornness of humanity.

GOD IS LOVE

Knowing the righteousness, jealousy, and patience of God's love are significant helps to people who wonder how hell can coexist with God's love. Some people will continue to struggle with this reality, however. At the end of the day, hell still exists. At the end of the day, you know people who are there, or you know people who are going there, and it makes you sick to think about it. At the end of the day, you just can't figure out how the existence of hell could ever be a good thing.

The reason you can't figure it out is because it's not what you would do. If it were up to you, there would be no hell. If you were God, you would find a way for your loved ones to avoid hell altogether.

It's the same with all the objections to God's love. If you were God, you would run the universe without suffering, remove executions from the Old Testament, or eliminate confusing doctrines from the Bible. Whether the controversy is hell or something else, it just isn't the way you would do it, and the way God has done it confuses you. If that describes you, then I want to share two crucial truths you must believe to finally accept the way things really are. Are you ready?

Here's the first truth—*you are not God.*

And here is the second—*God is love.*

You are not God and God is love. This takes us back to the very beginning of this book and tests whether we really believe that message. God's very existence is love itself. The real and true God has love bound up with who he is. God doesn't know how to be unloving.

Sinful people like you and me tend to define love on our own apart from biblical categories. We make up our own definition of love based on our preferences, demands, and assumptions. After we decide what love must be, we insist that everything about God's love must fit into what we determined in advance. Because hell does not fit into our definition of love, we can't imagine how it could possibly coexist with God's love.

This approach is exactly wrong.

To understand love, we must take the opposite approach. We must approach the God who is love and discover what love is from him, on his terms, based on all that he says and does. God defines what love is. Whenever we discover an action of God that seems unloving, we can know for certain that the problem is with us and not with God. We must be willing to expand our definition of love to include anything and everything that God does. God is love, not us. And we really can trust him.

In the book of Genesis, God determined to destroy the cities of Sodom and Gomorrah. Abraham, concerned that God would do the wrong thing and punish people who don't deserve it, bargained with God to spare the cities for the sake of the righteous within them, finishing his plea with, "Shall not the Judge of all the earth do what is just?" (Genesis 18:25).

If you wonder how God's love and hell can go together, then the question you ultimately must ask yourself is this: *Shall not the Judge of all the earth do what is just?*

And before you answer, you need to consider that love does not define your existence like it does God's. *God is love.* Every day of your life has been a precious gift of his love lavished on you. He has rescued you countless times from dangers you aren't even aware of. He made the ultimate sacrifice of his one perfect Son to shield you from an eternity apart from him so that you could enjoy him forever.

God delights in you. God gives you wonderful things. God protects you. God loves you. "This is love, not that we have loved God but that he loved us" (1 John 4:10). You need to learn from God what love is. He does not need to learn from you.

Shall not the Judge of all the earth do what is just? Of course, he will! He doesn't know how to do anything else. He will do what is right with you. He will do what is right with the people you love. He will do what is right with everyone who has ever lived. *God is love,* and you can trust him—even with the existence of hell.

CHAPTER 9

Trusting in God's Love

*We have come to know and to believe
the love that God has for us.*

1 JOHN 4:16

*R*eal love reshapes you.

When my oldest son was just a little guy, he loved to sleep with three stuffed animals named Big Doggy (the largest dog), Little Doggy (the smallest), and Peaches (it's a long story). Of the three dogs his absolute favorite was Big Doggy. Every night he fell asleep with one arm stretched across his beloved dog, pressing it close to his chest. Now, after all these years, we still have Big Doggy, and when you look at him, there is a massive dip across his midsection that is the exact shape of my son's toddler-sized arm. My son's love pulled that animal into his own loving embrace until it was cast into a different form than it was before.

Real love reshapes you.

As you think about this reality, recall that someone in your life deeply loves you. A mom or dad, a husband or wife, a pastor or friend has taken time to know you. They have listened to you at length, and they understand you. They made investments in you and stood up for you. You know they love you. Those people are so rare that most people make it through life knowing only a few. Whoever those people are in your life, they have made a difference in you. They have made you better. It is impossible to encounter real love and stay the same.

What is true with people is ten trillion times truer with God. No one you have ever met loves you with the great love of God who delights in you, gives you the most wonderful gifts, and protects you forever from harm. God's love does something to you. It impacts you. It changes you. God's loving embrace presses around you and shapes you into something different than you were before. It is impossible truly to encounter the great love of God and remain the same.

Real love reshapes you. It reforms you. It makes you different than you used to be. Real love changes you.

The rest of this book explains how the great love that defines God's essence will transform your existence. Throughout the years of your life and into eternity, God's love will change everything about you. Once you know the love of God, it will be impossible to stay the same. It is inconceivable that any book could describe all that will be different about you when God changes you with his love. The rest of this book will focus on a few of the most crucial transformations God's love makes in you. We begin in this chapter by exploring how God's great love makes us people of great faith.

FAITH

Religious people talk about faith a lot. Someone describes another as "a man of great faith." We encourage people to "trust the Lord." We tell ourselves to "depend on God." We even call ourselves believers. All these expressions point to the same thing. Whenever we use language that encourages trust, reliance, belief, or dependence, we are talking about the centrality of faith. We can talk about how faith defines someone in two ways.

There is a sense in which faith is a passive thing. In this sense, faith doesn't do anything—it rests, depends, and looks to the work of another. We exhibit faith in this passive sense all the time. In the church I pastor, we have a strong, delightful, and faithful law enforcement officer named Rick paid to help keep me safe. When I am at church, I am free to do my job, enjoy our people, and focus on ministry. I am never concerned about what I would do if someone tried to hurt me because I trust Rick to do that.

Similarly, I am married to the best cook I have ever known. My faith in my wife to prepare dinner does not require me to cook one thing. I just show up at the table. In still another way, I was able to trust that the sun would come up today without doing anything to make it happen. Faith in the passive sense trusts another to work, to perform, and to accomplish without attempting that work yourself.

There is another sense, however, in which faith is a very active reality. An active faith in someone displays how convinced you are that they will accomplish the work you are trusting them to do. This kind of faith doesn't waver as it boldly looks to another. "Faith is the assurance of things hoped for, the conviction of things not seen" (Hebrews 11:1). Faith looks to another to accomplish something for you with full assurance and conviction.

Faith is the one thing you can do that is not something you do. It looks to another with full dependence and confidence, never trying to do the work you are trusting them to do. As people who know God, when we talk about faith, we usually focus on God or Jesus Christ. Our faith is in God. We believe in Jesus Christ.

But what is the work we are trusting God to do for us? When we rest in Jesus, what are we depending on him to do? I want to strengthen your faith in Jesus by applying everything we have talked about in this book to faith, your personal relationship of trust with the Lord.

FAITH IN GOD'S LOVE

We are called to trust in God, of course, but how do we take that statement beyond a platitude? It sounds good, but it doesn't tell us much. Because it does not tell us what we are trusting God to do, we must say more. Biblical faith trusts in God's love. You have the kind of faith in God that he requires when you have faith in his great love for you.

This faith in God's love is the kind of faith that David had: "But I have trusted in your steadfast love" (Psalm 13:5). It was the faith of the apostle Paul: "The life I now live in the flesh I live by faith in the Son of God, who loved me and gave himself for me" (Galatians 2:20). This was also the kind of faith the apostle John had and wanted for all believers: "We have come to know and to believe the love that God has for us" (1 John 4:16).

We have seen the three demonstrations of God's love: to delight, to give, and to protect. Throughout Scripture, when God's people trust him, they are trusting in these three concrete demonstrations of his love. God's people in the exodus had faith that he would give them the land because he delighted in them (Numbers 14:8). You trust in God because he promises to lavish you with wonderful gifts (Psalm 84:11–12). The apostle Paul trusted in God to be his protector from all evil (2 Timothy 1:12). One of the most definitive passages on faith in the entire Bible clarifies faith's necessity and result: "Without faith it is impossible to please him, for whoever would draw near to God must believe that he exists and that he rewards those who seek him" (Hebrews 11:6).

God will never be pleased with you unless you rest in his ability to do work for you that you can never do on your own. Your trust exhibits your strong confidence in his desire and ability to reward you. You believe that he wants to give you wonderful things. Pleasing God requires trusting that he loves you.

One of the great examples of faith in the Bible is a man named Abram. The great love of God found this man and transformed everything about him. Abram's first experience of God's loving embrace happened in his hometown of Ur when he heard the voice of God: "Go from your country and your kindred and your father's house to the land that I will show you" (Genesis 12:1).

I have shared my experience of lying in an operating room and experiencing the love of God. If that seemed like an unusual way to encounter God's love, then Abram's experience is utterly bizarre. The shock of this command is found in the way ancient people lived. They were born, lived, and died in their town with very few ever venturing more than a few miles away. God asked Abram to pack up and travel to a completely different part of the world in a premodern age without phones, Google searches, or maps.

This request was abrupt and strange—even scary—but it was a demonstration of God's loving embrace. You see the loving nature of this request in God's promise, "I will make of you a great nation, and I will bless you and make your name great, so that you will be a blessing. I will bless those who bless you, and him who dishonors you I will curse, and in you all the families of the earth will be blessed" (Genesis 12:2–3).

God's words concretely demonstrate the three expressions of God's love. God's *delight* in Abram is seen in choosing to reveal himself to this one man out of all the people on the earth (Genesis 12:1). God's *gifts* to Abram are seen in the gifts of a promise of blessing and the fulfilment of that promise in personal blessing, a marvelous reputation, and blessing to all the families of the earth (Genesis 12:2). God's commitment to *protect* Abram from his enemies is seen in extending a curse to anyone who dishonors him (Genesis 12:3).

When the love of God came to Abram in this way, it changed everything about him. The first change was a residential change. Abram's home changed from Ur to Palestine. Abram's role in the world would also change. His destiny was changed from a forgettable man in a far corner of the world to becoming the father of many nations and a blessing to all the peoples of the world. Even his name would change from Abram to Abraham—the great man of faith.

Abraham heard God's command and the logic behind it, and the Bible records his very straightforward response: "So Abram went, as the LORD had told him" (Genesis 12:4). Abraham obeyed God. But he did not merely obey. Abraham did not just do what he was told. His was the obedience of faith: "By faith Abraham obeyed when he was called to go out to a place that he was to receive as an inheritance. And he went out, not knowing where he was going" (Hebrews 11:8). Abraham had faith in God's love to do all he had promised.

The classic example of Abraham's great faith came at a time of despair. He was old, well past the age that a typical man could consider being a father, and Abraham still had no child. He had believed God, moved across the known world, and staked everything on God's promise to provide an heir, but at his age, having children was physically impossible.

Then, late on a dark night, God visited Abraham and made the grandest of promises. God promised Abraham far more than even a single child. He promised Abraham that one day his offspring would be so numerous as to be uncountable: "Look toward heaven, and number the stars, if you are able to number them . . . So shall your offspring be" (Genesis 15:5). A promise of descendants as numerous as the innumerable stars was another demonstration of God's love, and Abraham "believed the LORD" (Genesis 15:6). He had faith. Abraham trusted in God's love for him.

Abraham's confidence in God was tested in one of the greatest stories of faith in human history. God kept his word and expressed his love to Abraham in the precious gift of a son. This boy, Isaac, was the one that God promised to be the person who would carry God's blessings to the entire earth. Through Isaac, God had told Abraham, all the families of the earth were going to be blessed. Then—in a breathtaking and horrifying surprise—God commanded Abraham to kill Isaac. It was a stunning development.

Abraham was ordered to sacrifice the boy God had promised, the boy Abraham had waited for, and the boy on whom depended the blessings of all the families of the earth. Abraham must have felt at least like Martha and Mary when their brother Lazarus died. God's demand seemed out of step with everything else he had said. It didn't make any sense.

But Abraham obeyed. Abraham took his boy up to the top of a mountain. As he arranged the altar, his hands were filled with wood, and his heart was filled with pain. Then, in a desperate display of obedience, Abraham grasped Isaac, bound him with rope, and placed his son on the altar instead of an animal. His body shook with sobs, and his hand quivered in terror as he extended the knife above his son's precious body.

Then, at just the right moment, God called to Abraham from heaven, "Do not lay your hand on the boy or do anything to him, for now I know that you fear God, seeing you have not withheld your son, your only son, from me" (Genesis 22:12). It had all been a test. Just like God did with Martha, Mary, and Lazarus, and just like he does with you, so he did with Abraham. God tested Abraham with suffering to discern whether Abraham loved God or God's gifts. Abraham passed the test.

Abraham was able to pass the test and endure the grief because he trusted in the great love of God: "By faith Abraham, when he was tested, offered up Isaac . . . He considered that God was able even to raise him from the dead" (Hebrews 11:17, 19). Abraham trusted that God would keep his loving promise, even if it required the gift of a resurrection.

Many people read this account with horror that God would make such a request. They are disgusted that Abraham would even consider it. The problem they have is not with God or with Abraham, but the problem lies deep in their own heart. Their disgust shows they do not trust the loving character of God as Abraham did.

When doubters encounter hard words from God, their instinct is to distrust his compassionate character and tender intentions. Believing they know more about love than God himself, they refuse to follow his difficult demands and miss the great blessing God has waiting on the other side of faithfulness.

This was not Abraham's problem: "No unbelief made him waver concerning the promise of God, but he grew strong in his faith as he gave glory to God, fully convinced that God was able to do what he had promised" (Romans 4:20–21). Abraham trusted in the great love of God. When he didn't understand God's actions, he trusted God's heart. Abraham's faithfulness led him to know more of the love of God than he knew before his trial, and he became a source of blessing to all who hear about his test of faith. Everyone who reads his example is encouraged to greater faith in God's great love.

You can be like Abraham. In your life, God is going to ask you to do things that overwhelm you. Things you cannot understand. Maybe there are commands in the Bible that seem impossible for you to obey. Perhaps God has placed challenges in your life that seem impossible to overcome. When you face these obstacles, you must be willing to rearrange your assumptions. God will never act in your life to be hateful. When God intervenes in your life, it is to show his love. You need to trust this. Abraham's life proves that when we can't understand God's difficult demands, we can always trust his loving heart.

A FAILURE OF FAITH IS A FAILURE OF LOVE

Abraham is known through history as the man of faith because his life was characterized by trust in the great love of God. Nobody is perfect, however—not even Abraham. Though Abraham demonstrated remarkable faith, he also had his fair share of significant lapses in faith. On two separate occasions, Abraham lied and said that his beautiful wife was his sister out of fear that other men would murder him to be with her (Genesis 12:10–16; 20:1–7). On another occasion, Abraham, at the instigation of his wife, married another woman and had a child with her after living in the land of promise for ten years with no child of their own (Genesis 16:1–6). These tragic sins of lying, fear, adultery, and polygamy brought grief and pain into the lives of Abraham and Sarah as well as many others.

All of Abraham's sins were driven by a failure of faith in God's love. Abraham never needed to fear for his life. He didn't need to lie and say Sarah was his sister. He certainly didn't need to enter a sinful sexual relationship with another woman to force an heir. These sins were Abraham's efforts to provide for and protect himself. He was not trusting in God's love. He forgot what he had remembered in the faithful test with Isaac, that God's love will never fail. Abraham's worst moments were fueled by a failure of faith in the great love of God.

This reality is visible throughout the entire Bible. Exodus provides another example when God promised his people that he would give them the land of Israel and protect them from the enemies living in the country at that time. The people experienced a failure of faith when they said, "Why is the LORD bringing us into this land, to fall by the sword? Our wives and our little ones will become a prey" (Numbers 14:3). They impugn God's character and make false assumptions about his involvement in their lives. Though God actively showed his people love with his promise of provision and protection, when the Israelites heard about enemies in the land, they gave in to their fears instead of trusting God's love.

God was appalled by their response. "The LORD said to Moses, 'How long will this people despise me? And how long will they not believe in me, in spite of all the signs that I have done among them?'" (Numbers 14:11). God identifies their sin as a failure of faith, *How long will they not believe in me?* They refuse to believe, even though he protected them from the plagues, delivered them out of Egypt, provided food and water in the desert, and rescued them through the Red Sea. God had demonstrated great love in countless ways, yet the people wouldn't believe.

God disapproved of their faith failures in the strongest terms, calling it an act of hatred, *How long will this people despise me?* When God lavishes his love on us and we respond by doubting that love, it is a clear act of hatred on our part against the God of great love. It breaks his heart and arouses his displeasure.

Another example of a failure of faith in God's love happened in Jesus's ministry. When Jesus was traveling with his disciples across the Sea of Galilee, a powerful storm broke out and terrified everyone on board except Jesus, who was sound asleep. The storm was so serious that it even drove Jesus's fishermen-disciples into a panic. Frustration was added to fear as they observed Jesus sleeping through all this danger.

In the chaos, they roused him from sleep with a question, "Teacher, do you not care that we are perishing?" (Mark 4:38). Jesus heard the question, arose from his nap, and with the same ease of wiping the sleep from his eyes unleashed glorious and breathtaking power. He spoke to the sea: "Peace! Be still" (Mark 4:39).

That was all it took. When the wind and rain heard the voice of their maker, they did as they were told. The storm stopped, and calm stretched through the clear night air.

After stopping the storm, Jesus turned to his disciples in the newfound quiet of the night and asked, "Why are you so afraid? Have you still no faith?" (Mark 4:40).

The Son of God had little concern about a storm on the sea but had great concern about the hearts of his disciples. These men had seen his love and compassion shown to the crowds, to sick people, and to them. Yet in a storm, fear drove out faith, and they questioned the care of Christ.

Scripture has many more examples of this kind of thing, but the examples you are most familiar with are the ones in your own heart. In your anger against someone who has mistreated you, you fail to trust God's loving commitment to vindicate you and lash out in vengeful rage. In the sorrow of your suffering, you do not trust God to comfort you with his love but despair of ever experiencing joy. In your lust, you fail to trust God to love you with the gifts you need at just the right time and grab onto sexual delights that he has forbidden. The tension of financial stress leads you to fretfulness instead of confidence in God to provide. Your faith fails, and you doubt God's love for you. You respond to perfect love with doubt and hate. God's ancient question to Moses rings in our ears, *How long will this people despise me?*

When we come to our senses and realize our failures of faith, we have two helpful ways to respond. The first is to remember Abraham. Abraham is the great standard of faithfulness even though he experienced serious lapses in faith. When faith failed, he placed himself in danger and his wife at risk, and he dishonored his God. None of Abraham's individual failures in faith changed God's judgment that he was fundamentally faithful. The glorious lesson for you to learn is that it is not the amount of faith but the presence of it that matters. Jesus says faith the size of a mustard seed is all you need (Luke 17:6).

When you realize faith failures in your life, there is a second way to respond. You must keep trusting in God. Abraham is a lesson here as well. The reason he is remembered as a man of faith is because, even when his faith failed, he always turned again to trust in the Lord. The most important reality about faith is not where it comes from but where it is going. The person on whom faith is focused is far more important than the person who has the faith. Our faith is focused on the God of great love. Our faith might not be infinite, but God's love is. Our faith may fail, but his love never will. When you are tempted to despair, take your eyes off yourself and focus the eyes of your faith on the God of great love.

THE ATTRIBUTE ON WHICH THE CHURCH STANDS OR FALLS

The good news about the love of God in Jesus Christ is that Jesus protects us from all our sins—even our failures of faith. One of the most important places in the Bible where we see this is in Romans 3:21–25:

> But now the righteousness of God has been manifested apart from the law, although the Law and the Prophets bear witness to it—the righteousness of God through faith in Jesus Christ for all who believe. For there is no distinction: for all have sinned and fall short of the glory of God, and are justified by his grace as a gift, through the redemption that is in Christ Jesus, whom God put forward as a propitiation by his blood to be received by faith.

Three incredible truths from these words help us know how to respond to God's love with faith.

The first truth is that the blood of Jesus Christ shed on the cross is a loving gift from God himself. God shows his love for us in the gifts he gives, and the most precious gift he has given is the life of his Son. Romans 3 says the reason the blood of Jesus is so precious is because it acquires another gift, propitiation.

This sophisticated theological expression refers to one of the most practical and wonderful gifts in all the universe. Our sin brings about God's righteous wrath and must be punished. When Jesus died as a perfect sacrifice on the cross, he took the punishment of sinners even though he was righteous. His innocent sacrifice in the place of guilty sinners satisfied God's righteous wrath. Propitiation means that God's wrath has been satisfied by Jesus, and he no longer responds to our sin with anger.

The second truth from Romans 3 is that Jesus's propitiation of the wrath of God leads to justification for sinners. Justification is another sophisticated theological term packed with life-changing meaning. Justification happens when God declares that a sinner is righteous. The truth of justification has been the source of tremendous controversy throughout church history because people question how God can declare a sinner to be righteous. If sinners are not righteous, then how can God declare them to be?

The answer comes in the fact that Jesus's blood secures the propitiation of God's wrath. On the cross, God treated Jesus as though he lived the life of a sinner, pouring out his wrath on his Son to satisfy divine justice. After Jesus's blood propitiated God's wrath, God now turns to sinful people and treats sinners as though they lived Jesus's life. Justification is the declaration from God that Jesus has changed their status, and they now possess the righteousness of Christ.

The final truth from Romans 3:21–25 and the one that connects it so crucially to this chapter on faith in God's love is that all the blessings of propitiation and justification purchased by the blood of Jesus become the property of believers through faith. Paul says twice in the verse that these blessings are received by faith. These extravagant gifts of propitiation and justification belong to anyone who believes.

Your sins are paid for, God's wrath toward you is diverted, and you are declared to be as righteous as Jesus himself when you believe that these things belong to you. If you can't believe God would do this for you, if you despise his love, then these blessings will never be yours. But, with all your heart, if you believe in the great love of God to justify you, then he can, he will, and he has.

One of the most important men in world history started out as an obscure German monk. His name was Martin Luther, and he was heartbroken. He read in the book of Romans about the righteousness of God, and it made him despair to the depths of his soul. He knew God's righteousness was infinite and his own was nonexistent. He was in spiritual agony regarding how a sinner like him could ever be acceptable to a God of spotless moral purity.

He worked hard to press purity into his life through moral strain and religious effort. He prayed fervently, read the Bible, and stripped himself of physical comforts. Nothing worked. He could find no way to cleanse himself of his moral stains.

Then, suddenly, everything changed. Luther discovered that sinners can never earn God's righteousness. He learned God's righteousness is a gift that he gives to those who trust in Jesus. Righteousness is not something a sinner can do—it is something God must give. This gift of righteousness is the property of everyone who believes.

Luther's personal discovery of the glorious truth of justification changed his life and changed the world. Luther opposed anyone who challenged the importance of justification by faith alone because it was the only way that people could be accepted by God. Justification was so important to Luther that he declared justification to be the article on which the church stands or falls. His point was that there can be no faithful church without the conviction that God's righteousness is something that must be given as a gift and received by faith.

It is true that the church cannot exist without the truth of justification. But there is something even more fundamental to the church's existence than the doctrine of justification. Justification is a crucial gift from God. That indispensable gift of declared righteousness comes as the result of a prior gift from God, the sacrifice of Jesus, which propitiates the wrath of God.

This most precious gift from God flows from a disposition in his heart. God loves his people so much that he desires to give them wonderful things including his Son, who died in their place to propitiate God's wrath so that he could justify them with a declaration that they are like Jesus himself. All these gifts are marks of great love in the heart of God. If justification is the article on which the church stands or falls, then love is the *attribute* on which the church stands or falls. God's heart of love makes justification possible. If you love justification as you should, you must adore God's heart of love that makes it possible.

When Christians say we believe in faith alone, we are saying sinners can do nothing to earn their salvation. We are saying that we trust in Jesus to pay for our sins with his blood. We are saying that we trust in God's declaration that we are righteous. We are also saying we trust God's great love to grant these realities. We are saying that we have faith in Jesus alone because we have faith in the great love of God.

CHAPTER 10

Loving as We Have Been Loved

We love because he first loved us.
1 JOHN 4:19

You can tell a lot about someone by what they tell you to do. Years ago, I was the new pastor in a small church and arrived late to work after an appointment at the hospital with my wife and newborn son. As I walked into the church office, I heard the secretary lying to someone on the phone that I was in a meeting and couldn't be disturbed.

When I asked her about it, she admitted the lie, explaining that the influential church member on the phone would have been unhappy to know I was not in the office. She defended the dishonesty, saying this was the way the previous pastor had asked her to respond. As I asked more questions about this man, I learned that he was thoroughly corrupt. He stole money, lied, made sexual advances at her, and had a raging temper. His immoral demand that she lie for him was only one demonstration of his character. For good or for ill, you can tell what is in someone's heart by the demands they make.

It is significant that when Jesus is asked what the greatest commandment is in the Bible, he responds with a twofold answer, "You shall love the Lord your God with all your heart and with all your soul and with all your strength and with all your mind, and your neighbor as yourself" (Luke 10:27). The Jewish leaders of Jesus's day wanted to know which of the 613 commandments in the Old Testament he believed was the most important. In an instant, Jesus gave an authoritative summary that came with the sanction of heaven. The most important command in the Bible is love.

This response should surprise you because it is so utterly out of the ordinary. Most people with authority and influence would not say this. In this horrible world, most leaders issue commands that are good for them without caring whether they harm you. We live in a world of hateful people issuing hateful commands.

This is not what Jesus does. Though he is the king of the universe and though he could say anything he wants, when asked to boil everything down to one command, he shows it's all about love. God's commands are directed at loving him and others.

If what people tell you to do tells you about who they are, then this command tells us wonderful things about God. It underlines God's loving character. It makes all the sense in the world that the God who is the very definition of love would issue love as the most fundamental command to his people. These words do more than underline God's nature. These words also tell us what God wants. God has drawn near to his people in love. He has delighted in us, given us wonderful things, and protected us from harm. Now this great God of love commands that we behave toward him and others the way he has behaved toward us.

God's command to love is an expression of his desire for relationship with us. What is amazing about this is that God doesn't need you to have a fulfilling relationship of love. God has perfect fellowship among the members of the Trinity—Father, Son, and Spirit. God is not lonely and does not need a relationship with his sinful creation. But he does *want* a relationship with us. God's desire for relationship leads to his command of love.

Some people get nervous when we start talking about commands and obedience. I'll have more to say about this in the following chapter, but, for now, if it makes you nervous to talk about obeying commands, then consider Jesus's words to be an invitation summoning you to live a life of love. The demand to love is a request to respond to God's loving embrace of you by embracing him in your love. It is a call to embrace others in your love.

The call to follow Jesus is a call to escape from the hateful and selfish demands of people in the world. To follow Jesus means you don't have to hate, you don't have to cut someone off in traffic, you don't have to humiliate people on social media, you don't have to bark at your server at dinner, write that nasty email, demean your husband, or scream at your kids. You also don't have to be angry at God, doubting and accusing him. Following Jesus empowers your escape from the confines of this nasty world collapsing under the weight of its own hatred. You can live by Jesus's kingdom rule of love. That kingdom is so wonderful and glorious that when you ask the king what he wants everybody to do, he gives a one-word command: love.

We cannot obey this command on our own. As sinners, we are

hateful and cannot participate in the glorious kingdom of love. We need help and power to turn from the hatefulness in our hearts to participate in the great and glorious kingdom of love. This help and power is just what Jesus offers.

Jesus loves us by gifting us with the ability to obey God's command to love. The life, death, and resurrection of Jesus for all who believe in him creates love in those who receive it: "We love because he first loved us" (1 John 4:19). Through Christ, God's love has been poured into our hearts (Romans 5:5). Because God is love, all love comes from God (1 John 4:7), and so when followers of Christ love, they are not demonstrating their own love but God's love overflowing into their hearts (1 John 3:17). God places his love in us and transforms us into loving people.

Real love reshapes you.

One of the most wonderful women in the Bible was caught up in this mighty current of God's great love. She encountered Jesus at a dinner party in the home of a religious big shot named Simon. Jesus was the most famous man in the country at the time, so having him at the party was like hosting a Hollywood superstar.

Simon was feeling good about his fancy party and his famous guests. While all the good, sophisticated, and important people were trying to enjoy their nice dinner, this woman, who was seen by Simon as morally suspect, unsophisticated, and insignificant, showed up. Simon's fascination with his fancy party and his famous guests was interrupted by a great frustration.

This uninvited woman broke into the party and went directly to Jesus while he ate dinner. In those days, you didn't sit at the table in chairs but reclined on the floor at low tables with your feet pointed out away from the food. The woman approached Jesus in tears and immediately fell to the floor at his feet. Jesus's feet were likely dirty from walking through Palestine in sandals, so she began to clean them. She had no water or towel, so she used her tears and her hair. While she cleaned his feet, she also covered them in kisses. Once the cleaning and the kissing were completed, she emptied an expensive jar of ointment on his feet.

This was all incredibly distracting, and—to be honest—odd. This "woman of the city" was known to everyone as a sinner, and there are only a few unsavory options as to how she earned that reputation (Luke 7:37). Every guest present would have stopped eating their hummus and pita and directed suspicious glances at Jesus and the commotion unfolding on his side of the table.

We know that Simon, the host, was very suspicious. In his frustration over the unsightly scene unfolding at his lovely party, he was convinced that Jesus couldn't possibly be a godly man if he were allowing this kind of behavior in polite company. Yet Jesus knew exactly who this woman was.

He understood what she was doing in front of God and everybody, and he let her continue. And Jesus also knew who Simon was. When Jesus looked at the "bad" woman making a scene at his feet, and the "good" man hosting a swanky dinner party, he chose to challenge Simon, not the woman.

Jesus pointed out that the difference between the woman of the city and the man of religion was that she knew God and Simon didn't. Jesus corrected Simon for not doing what the woman was doing. Simon should have cleaned Jesus's feet, should have kissed Jesus, and should have anointed his feet. Yet Simon did none of these things, while the woman did. Jesus explains the simple difference between Simon and the woman with three words: "She loved much" (Luke 7:47).

Jesus's love changed this woman from sinful to lovely, freeing her to love in return. In her time and town, the people knew her as a sinner. But the love of God redefined everything about her. Today, this woman has been memorialized throughout history as a woman marked by devoted love for Jesus. She was completely reshaped and redefined by the great love of God. This same reality will be true for you.

LOVING GOD

One of the most amazing things God does with his love is give it to us.

When that love reaches our hearts, it reshapes them from places of hate to places of love. We need to know what that place of love looks like so we will recognize it when we get there. If we want to understand what our life of love looks like, a great place to start is with the definition of God's love that we have already seen. What does *our* love look like in comparison?

When you compare God's love and our love, you will find obvious differences between the love God shows to us and the love we show to him. Remember that God's love is his commitment as God to delight in you, to give you wonderful things, and to protect you from harm. We see that our love is different from God's love at the outset because our love does not come from within us.

Our love is the overflow of God's love poured into our hearts: *we love because he first loved us.* When God loves, it is an outpouring of who he is by nature. When we love, we also do it out of the overflow of who God is—not who we are. God's love is his love—rooted in who he is. Our love, however, is not our love, rooted in who we are, but is God's love, rooted in who he is.

This means that when we love rightly—not for selfish or sinful reasons—we act not out of our own nature but out of a new nature that God has given to those who trust in him. God gets credit for his love, but he also gets the credit for our love. This means the first evidence that the love of God has reached our hearts will be a spirit of faith and gratitude for what God has done in giving love that we so desperately needed but did not have until he granted it. "We have come to know and to believe the love that God has for us. God is love, and whoever abides in love abides in God, and God abides in him" (1 John 4:16).

Once this change occurs in our hearts, our love begins to experience some overlap with God's love. We begin to love as God loves. It is the nature of God's love to delight in his people, so anyone changed by the great love of God will begin to delight in God. This is a miraculous change.

Before we were embraced by the reshaping love of God, we denied God (Romans 1:21–23) and we hated God (Romans 1:30). We did not seek God (Romans 3:11). We were enemies of God (Romans 5:10). God's love for us changes all that, allowing us to begin to delight in him as he has delighted in us.

The wonderful woman at Jesus's feet remarkably demonstrates her new delight in God effected by the love God had for her. At one time she was known and defined by her love for sin. Now she is known by her love for Jesus. Delight in her heart for God causes her to seek Jesus. Disregarding the thoughts of people or the propriety of the moment, she flung herself at the feet of Jesus. Her tears are obvious evidence of her delight in Jesus. The woman's soul has been moved by great love, and her soft heart is producing tears of delight at this encounter with God.

This great love for God will belong to anyone encountering the great love of God. Does this delight belong to you? Do you long for God with a power that casts off restraint in worship of him? When was the last time you experienced a tender movement of your soul related to thoughts of God alone? Have you considered the great love of God demonstrated to you and experienced a sweet melting of your heart that produced tears? The strong love of God for you will produce a tenderness in your heart for him.

Our experience of love for God does not end with our internal experience of delight for God. Love toward God must also be demonstrated in our actions. As we recall the nature of God's love, we remember that God moves from an internal experience of delight to granting gifts to his loved ones and protecting them from harm. Here we see another difference between God's love and our love. People cannot give to God in the same way that God gives to us because God is always the giver of every good and perfect gift, and we are always the recipients.

While we often speak of giving God things like money and service, these gifts are simply a return on what God has already granted. It is the same when we talk about "protecting God" from harm. God is not threatened by any individual or group of people and so does not need defending.

There is a type of defense we engage in when God's people evangelize or interact with critics, answering objections against God and his Word. These actions, however, are far from anything that would ultimately be considered protection. We have no need to take up arms or the sword to defend the honor of God. Instead, we speak truth in love, praying that the Word of God will bring change to God's enemies.

Because God does not need us, we must think about our actions of love toward God in very different categories than we think of God's actions of love toward us. Even though God does not need our service, he still desires it. So, it is right for us to talk about our own devotion to God as a demonstration of our love for him. This devotion knows that everything we have is a gift from God and willingly returns everything we have received as an act of faithfulness to him.

The woman at the feet of Jesus embodies this devotion to God and his Son, Jesus. She gave everything she had to express her love for Jesus. She gave her time and her life as she sought Jesus out to love and serve him by washing his feet. She sacrificed her pride and reputation as this woman with a past disregarded snickers and sneers to express devotion to Jesus regardless of what people thought. She gave her wealth and possessions as she poured an expensive bottle of perfume on Jesus's feet that would, ultimately, be pierced out of his love for her. The woman's delight in Jesus led to devotion to give everything she had as an extravagant display of love.

Most people have far more things than this woman had while demonstrating their love for God far less. Ultimately your love for God must be demonstrated with action. Are you living a life of love for God? Do you realize that there is nothing you possess that you did not first receive from God? When was the last time you told a loved one the story of all God has done for you even though you were embarrassed about what they might say? How tightly is your fist clenched around financial resources that God has given you that you refuse to invest in his kingdom so others could know his love?

When God's love wraps itself around you, your life will increasingly display the marks of his great love. The first demonstration of this will be in your love for God. But you will demonstrate even more love than this.

LOVING OTHERS

The presence of hatred in your heart is evidence of an absence of God's love. The apostle Paul describes the life of everyone before they know God: "We ourselves were once foolish, disobedient, led astray, slaves to various passions and pleasures, passing our days in malice and envy, hated by others and hating one another" (Titus 3:3). These words describe our life before love. Malice means I want bad things for you. Envy means I want your good things for myself.

The apostle Paul provides a perfect explanation of hatred. You want others to have all your bad things, and you want all their good things. Before you know the God of love, your life is defined by hating other people and them hating you right back.

The reshaping love of God ultimately presses all the hatred from our hearts and eventually leaves no room for it to return. The apostle John describes the way it is: "Everyone who hates his brother is a murderer, and you know that no murderer has eternal life abiding in him" (1 John 3:15). Hatred inflicts spiritual death on another person. It is a way of wishing they weren't even alive. No person who has received God's gift of eternal life has a heart that hates the life of another. It is impossible to know the God who is the very definition of love and be characterized by hate.

Because hatred is such a terrible threat, we must be sure we know what it is before it rouses its horrible head in our heart. In a world spilling over with the worst kinds of hatred, we should assume that our standard of hatred is lower than the one God has made. We look at people who are destroying the reputations of people online, who are using their power to abuse weak people, who are stealing money from innocent victims, who are murdering one another—and much more. Then we think that because we are not doing those terrible things, we are not really hating people. God's standard for hatred, however, is a much higher standard than the world's standard.

Just after John's declaration that anyone who hates his brother is a murderer, he says, "If anyone has the world's goods and sees his brother in need, yet closes his heart against him, how does God's love abide in him?" (1 John 3:17). The presence of hatred is far more subtle than merely engaging in hateful acts that seek the tangible destruction of another person. Hatred is as subtle as failing to give help when someone is in need. Hatred is something that happens inside the heart of a person. It is the closing of your heart against another human being.

Think of your heart as a room with a door where you welcome people. For some people the door of your heart is wide open, you invite them in, you let them lounge on the furniture, you allow them to eat your food. For these people, your heart is open and welcoming. For others, you have a different attitude. You don't want to make room for them in your heart. They annoy you, and you want them out. You close the door of your heart to these people. This attitude of a closed heart is hatred, biblically defined, even if you never act out that hatred in terrible behaviors toward them.

The attitude of people touched by the love of God is an open heart for others: "By this we know love, that he laid down his life for us, and we ought to lay down our lives for the brothers" (1 John 3:16). The clearest portrait of God's great love is the sacrifice of Jesus for sinners. He opened his eternal heart of love and invited unrighteous people in. He gave his heart and his life for his people. When the love of Jesus flows into our heart, that love will spill out into the lives of others. To know Christ is to love others with the same love he has for us.

But only God *is* love.

Because our hearts are not infinite like God's, we will never be able to love infinitely. A fundamental distinction will always exist between the Creator, whose limitlessness allows him to love infinitely, and his creation, whose finitude places limits on our ability to love. It is impossible for us to love everyone or to love anyone with the infinity characterized by God. Being created and limited means we must make decisions about how to love others.

In my life there are constant demands to love and care for people. Because I am not God, I could never meet all these demands. I have limited time and energy and must choose how my acts of love can best be invested. For me that means I prioritize loving Jesus first. After him, I am committed to loving my family well. Finally, I am committed to loving the members of my church.

You live in a different context than I do and will have to make different choices. The crucial truth to remember is that, though you will have to decide how to invest your limited energies in loving others well, your inability to love everyone equally will never be driven by hatred for anyone. It will, instead, be driven by a desire to love as best you can given your creation limitations.

Regardless of our limitations, we all must grow in our love for others. This love for others will not always be easy or quick. When you know God, you will experience dramatic changes in the direction of increased love, but God's work of making you a more loving person will take your entire life. You will need to grow in wisdom regarding what love really is.

Throughout your life there will be setbacks as you seek to love well. You will struggle with the presence of hatred in your own life, and you will encounter people who are hard to love. Each of us will experience some people and some seasons when love is hard. When this happens, it helps to remember three things.

Remember Who People Are

You will encounter people who are hard to love. Sometimes they will be people you've known for a long time and with whom you have had a close relationship. You may live with them. Though you've had good times in the past, your relationship has fallen on hard times. This relationship could be an old friend, a parent, a spouse, or a child. When you know someone long enough, your relationship will eventually go through seasons of difficulty when the call to love feels more burdensome.

Sometimes you struggle to love people you just met or don't know very well. It may be that you don't know them well on purpose. You don't want to get to know them because they annoyed you from the beginning! Whoever you're finding hard to love and however long you've known them, some truths can help you love in the face of challenges.

You should remember the person that is hard for you to love is made in the image of God (Genesis 1:27). God made every single human being to reflect who he is. Whether the person is your precious spouse or a man in your congregation who smells funny, every person you encounter is a representative of God himself. Remembering this helps you love when it is hard because loving people is a way to love God through the people he has made.

It also helps to remember that loving people concretely demonstrates that you love Jesus. Jesus once described to his followers what their future judgment would be like. He describes a reward that will be bestowed on his faithful followers for giving Jesus food when he was hungry, water when he was thirsty, shelter when he was alone, clothing when he was naked, comfort when he was sick, and fellowship when he was in prison.

Jesus points out that his followers will be shocked to receive this reward, having no recollection of ever doing any of the things Jesus described. But Jesus explains, "Truly, I say to you, as you did it to one of the least of these my brothers, you did it to me" (Matthew 25:40). A concrete way to love and serve Jesus is to love and serve his people. When love is hard, this reminds us to look past the frustrating person, use the eyes of faith, and love each person as you would love Jesus.

Remember Who You Are

When people are hard to love, it is also good to remember that you can be annoying too. If you are tempted to focus on how annoying some people can be to you, I have bad news. You are a nuisance to others. Incredibly frustrating things about you that you may not see grate on people's nerves. You might be focused on enjoying your food and don't notice that you make loud noises when you chew. What you perceive as a desire to offer helpful advice may be considered as being too opinionated. Jokes you think are funny are greeted as annoying and insensitive. A desire for direct communication is received as harshness. All of us do things that are annoying. It is true of me. It is true of you.

What are we to do in a world where we are all living together with our mutual frustrations and irritations? God gives a much more loving alternative than the hateful world does. The apostle Paul tells us that in the face of frustrations, our attitude should be defined by "bearing with one another in love" (Ephesians 4:2).

When people do frustrating things, we bear it. We tolerate it. We get over it. This toleration of the faults of others isn't the kind that grits your teeth in frustration. No, we tolerate others *in love*. We are happy about it. When someone is doing the thing that grates on our nerves, we remember we do things that get on their nerves too. We remember that we want them to love us when we are frustrating. We smile, we tolerate their weaknesses, and we wrap them in a warm and tender embrace of love.

Unfortunately, people are far worse than annoying. They are also sinful. Sin is different than weakness. We are told to bear with weaknesses. We are supposed to seek reconciliation and restoration when people are guilty of sin (2 Corinthians 13:11). As important as restoration is, there will be times in this broken world when it does not happen. This raises the issue of enemies that we discussed earlier under the category of God's loving protection. Unfortunately, we all have enemies. We all have people who persist in cruelly mistreating us, even when we have done nothing wrong or have sought to correct our wrongs.

The presence of enemies is no exception to God's law of love. On the contrary, Jesus himself commands, "Love your enemies and pray for those who persecute you" (Matthew 5:44). The demand to love your enemies is one of the hardest in Scripture. It requires that regardless of the cruelty of mistreatment, we seek to have an open heart and maintain a practical willingness to help if our enemy needs it (1 John 3:17), we refuse to allow a root of bitterness to spring up (Hebrews 12:15), we are always willing to be reconciled (Ephesians 4:32), and we refuse to mistreat our enemies as they have mistreated us (Matthew 7:12).

There are times when this will feel impossible. There are some enemies who have mistreated you in such dramatic ways that possessing a heart of love for them feels unthinkable. When this happens, remember that no one alive has ever mistreated you as much as you have mistreated God in your sin. Regardless of your offensive sin, God still loves you. "God shows his love for us in that while we were still sinners, Christ died for us" (Romans 5:8). A few verses later, Paul says, "While we were enemies we were reconciled to God by the death of his Son" (Romans 5:10).

When God asks you to bring your enemies into your loving embrace, he is not asking you to do anything he hasn't done for you. He is not asking you to do anything he won't help you to accomplish as you are increasingly reshaped by his embrace of great love.

Remember What Your Love Proves

The final reality we must remember in loving when it is hard is what our love for others proves. Jesus says, "By this all people will know that you are my disciples, if you have love for one another" (John 13:35). Sometimes Christians believe the only way they can prove their faithfulness to Jesus is by the truths they confess. While a defense of truth is crucial, it is also possible for this to become divisive. Well-intended people can defend truth in ways that are harsh, cruel, and harmful. Our defense of the truth can very quickly get focused on us, what we know, and how much of it we know.

A defense of the truth without love is harmful. "'Knowledge' puffs up, but love builds up" (1 Corinthians 8:1). We must match our love of the truth with our love for people. When Jesus commanded his followers to prove their faithfulness to him with love, he knew he was talking to Christians who would disagree about buckets of crucial realities: who is allowed to be baptized, who is qualified to serve as a pastor or deacon, what the Bible teaches about divine sovereignty and human freedom, what songs we should sing when we're together, how to spend ministry money in the best way, and 927 other things!

In the midst of all those important disagreements, Jesus insists that people will know you're his disciples if you have love for one another. In a world as hateful as this one, it is crucial that people see something different from those of us who follow the God of great love. They must see us following him with resolute determination. They must see us willing to defend the great truths of the faith. But they must see us doing all of this in a spirit of love. The only encounter of God's loving embrace that some people may experience is the one that comes through us. Our demonstration of care may be the very thing God uses to reshape them into a life of love that will change their eternity.

Do you remember the remarkable woman who expressed such tender devotion to Jesus at the home of Simon when she washed his feet with her tears and hair and anointed them with oil? What is apparent in the narrative is the love she had for God, just like we have been discussing in this chapter. What is not so obvious is her love for people since the only person we see her interacting with is Jesus. There are examples in her story of love for people, however. For example, she was loving *you*. Thousands of years after her tender act of love, her example is motivating and inspiring you to love the Lord the way this woman did. The woman was also loving Simon as she offended him with her behavior. She demonstrated love he should have had for Jesus but did not.

It is true that she did not know about you or focus on Simon because she was focused on Jesus. That is actually the point. The woman loved the people at the party by exemplifying love for God through their scoffing. She loved you the same way as she set an example to follow even when that example might have been embarrassing. She did all that simply by focusing on Jesus. You love people best when you love God most.

Some people confuse love for people with fear of people. Often, our deferential and friendly behavior toward others does not grow out of love for them but out of fear of what they will think about us, fear about what they will say, fear about how they will receive us. To be guided by love in our interactions with people is a mark of the grace of Jesus. To be guided by fear is a mark of sin in our life. The two can be very hard to distinguish. You can tell the difference if your desire to defer to others leads you to sin against God or compromise your witness for Christ. Whenever you do this, people might think your actions are motivated by love, but they really are motivated by fear.

There is a reason why Jesus put God before people when he presents the greatest commandment. It is not possible to love people well unless you have loved God first. The great love of God will reshape you into a person who will love him in return. The more you are reshaped by his love, the more you will become like him by loving others—even when it's hard. One of the greatest blessings of God's love is the gift of his own ability to love.

CHAPTER 11

Obeying the God of Love

*Whoever keeps his word, in him truly
the love of God is perfected.*
1 JOHN 2:5

God's loving embrace reshapes you and presses you into a life of love that will change everything about you. Nothing will stay the same. God's love transforms you into a person of great faith. His love fashions you into a person that loves God and others. His love also changes you into an obedient person.

Jesus binds love and obedience together into an inseparable package. He says, "If you love me, you will keep my commandments" (John 14:15). This revolutionary statement changes everything we once thought about obeying God's law. Jesus's words make it impossible to separate our love for God and our obedience to God.

Because Jesus's words are true, we can say with certainty that obedience to God's law is an act of relational love.

Yet many view obedience the opposite way. They see obedience as burdensome and—if not hateful—then at least corrosive of a loving focus on relationship. Because Jesus takes an opposite view from so many on the nature of love and obedience, we have some explaining to do.

Let me begin by observing that what is true in our relationship with God is true in our other relationships as well. Some form of legal code governs every loving relationship you have. Marriage is a great example. In loving marriages, the sexual relationship is an exclusive one. People who are devoted to their spouses know that being sexually intimate with other people is a hateful act that undermines marital love.

Rules also govern the relationship of love between parents and children. Children must honor, respect, and obey their parents. Children behave hatefully against their parents and weaken relational love when they behave with disrespect and disobedience.

Unspoken rules also exist in your friendships when, for example, you know that it is hateful and unloving to speak badly about your friends behind their back. In every relationship there are behaviors that demonstrate love and others that demonstrate hatefulness. You know those behaviors by the rules of the relationship. In any relationship, showing love means following rules.

Even though rules manifest love in every relationship and even though Jesus says, *if you love me, you will keep my commandments*, it makes many uncomfortable to speak of obedience to God's law as a manifestation of our love for him. If you are nervous at the thought of law-keeping as a demonstration of relational love toward God, the reason is because you do not like obedience to God's law. If you do not like obedience to God's law, there is an important reason why. That reason has to do with a crucial reality in the attitude and actions of every person who has ever lived.

Every human being alive is a law keeper. You can't help it. The laws we keep depend on the master we have. The Bible uses the powerful metaphor of slavery to explain that everyone alive is bound to a master and will always follow the commands of that master. Ultimately, only two choices exist for who your master might be (Romans 6:16). Your master could be yourself and your sin. If that is true, then you are enslaved to sin—you will always faithfully obey your master, and sin will characterize your life. The other option is to have God as your master. If God is your master, righteous obedience to his law will characterize your life.

The bad news, as the image of slavery suggests, is that on our own, we are bound to sin as our master and never obey God. Jesus says, "Truly, truly, I say to you, everyone who practices sin is a slave to sin" (John 8:34). The reason it is a source of discomfort to talk about obedience to God's law as an act of relational love is because we do not love God or his law. Instead, we love ourselves and follow the demands of our own desires. We are enslaved to the wrong master and enamored with the wrong law.

But there is good news too. Though we love our sin, God loves us. In love, God's love is greater than our sin, so he sent his Son to die for our sin. Once we are set free from our sin by trusting in Jesus Christ, we have God as our new master and are bound to him (Romans 6:17–18). It is the loving work of Jesus to set us free from sin: "So if the Son sets you free, you will be free indeed" (John 8:36).

The love of Jesus releases our hearts that have been enslaved to the harsh master of sin and gives us God as our new, gracious master. Our hearts are changed so that we have a new love for God and for doing what he wants us to do. When Jesus says, *If you love me, you will keep my commandments*, he is making an unbreakable promise.

The reshaping power of God's great love transforms us into people who obey the law of God. God's love changes us from being people who break his law to people who keep it. Our obedience flowing from the overflow of God's great love is crucial in our relationship to him.

GOD'S LOVE AND LAW

The inseparable bond between love and obedience means that law is intrinsically loving. The law of God reveals the love of God. This reality is true in the other relationships of love I mentioned. The rule of marital faithfulness is intrinsically loving, allowing me the opportunity to forsake all women out of loving devotion to my wife. What is true of laws regarding human relationships are true of the law of God as well. God's law reveals God's love. God's law reveals his loving character, demonstrates his love for us, shows how we can love him, and provides an opportunity for us to love others.

God's Law Reveals His Loving Character

If the kind of commands people give reflect their heart, then laws are never arbitrary, but always reveal character. A generous man will give generous commands. A harsh person will give harsh commands. One who is unwise will issue foolish commands. There is never a separation between the character of a person and the commands they issue.

Because God is defined by great love, his commands will always reflect his loving character. It is possible to see the great love of God in all of God's commands, but one example of God's love is seen in his clear and repeated commands against murder. Murder is sinful because it is the ultimate assault against human beings, who are God's creation made precious by being made in his image (Genesis 9:6).

Jesus traces the command against murder down into the roots of anger and hatred in the hearts of those who kill (Matthew 5:21–26). Because murder begins in the hearts of hateful people, we know that the command to preserve life begins in the heart of God, who loves life and desires to preserve it rather than end it through hateful measures.

This command against murder is only one example, but there are many others. Commands against adultery demonstrate God's heart of faithfulness. Commands to give to the needy point to God's love for the weak. Commands against gossip reveal God's concern to protect the reputation of his people. You get the point. God's law is loving because it reveals the character of the God who is love.

God's Law Reveals God's Love for Us

God's commands do more than reflect his loving character; they also demonstrate his love for us. It is important to acknowledge that God's commands are an expression of his love for us. So often we evaluate those commands in an opposite and dangerous way. In our frustration over a lack of desire and ability to do what God has said, we curse God and his commands when the problem actually lies with us. Every word from God is good and is a loving expression of the great love of God. We can see the demonstration of this love for us in both a positive and negative way.

Positively, God's love for us is seen in his law through the invitation it offers to participate in the life of God. Relationships never work when the rules that require their operation are not followed.

No wife wants to be married to a philanderer. No boss can employ someone who is repeatedly insubordinate. A perfectly righteous God can have no relationship with a thoroughly disobedient sinner (Revelation 21:8). God tells us what his standards are for obedience so we can relate to him as we should. Because God is not required to tell us how to relate to him, it demonstrates his love for us when he explains the standards for our relationship. Like the vows made by a married couple on their wedding day, the law of God sets out the terms of our relationship with God.

Negatively, God's love for us warns us away from sin. This is the opposite of the positive function I just described. In that positive sense, God's law invites us to participate with him in a righteous relationship. In this negative sense, God's law warns us what will happen if we go our own way and fail to live righteously before God: "Cursed be everyone who does not abide by all things written in the Book of the Law, and do them" (Galatians 3:10). God loves us with his law by graciously warning us of the terrible fate that awaits anyone who does not conform to his righteousness through obedience to his commands.

Jesus says that anyone who loves him keeps his commands. Conversely, the prophet Isaiah states that our sins separate us from God and destroy our relationship with him (Isaiah 59:2). The fact that law keeping leads to closeness with God and law breaking leads to separation from him means that all our responses to all of God's laws are intrinsically relational. One of God's commands that most obviously demonstrates the relational nature of God's love are his commands to pray. God gives a clear command that his people are supposed to pray and that obedience to this command furthers a real and dynamic relationship of love (Luke 18:1–8).

When you see the relational nature of the command to pray, it points to the positive function of God showing us how to relate to him. The Bible is clear that when we draw near to God in prayer, he will draw near to us (James 4:8). The command to pray as an invitation to loving relationship also points to the negative function of warning us off sin. God clarifies the negative consequences of not drawing near to him in prayer by declaring, "You do not have, because you do not ask" (James 4:2). God's law does not just reveal his character as the God of great love but expresses his great desire for a relationship with us.

Obedience to God's Law Demonstrates Our Love for God

Another way we see God's love in God's law is the opportunity it provides to love him. God's law reveals his character and expresses his desire for a relationship with his people. Now, we get to see that when we obey his law, it is our opportunity to respond in that relationship of love with love of our own. Remember that Jesus says, *if you love me, you will keep my commandments.* In Jesus's view, obedience is an opportunity to demonstrate our love for God.

It is impossible to love another in relationship without honoring the rules of that relationship. If a woman says she loves her husband but goes to a hotel room with another man, she is not telling the truth. If a father says he loves his son but physically abuses his boy, he is a liar. In the same way, our disobedience shows our true heart of opposition to God. When we obey God, however, it proves that we love him.

The command against stealing (Exodus 20:15) demonstrates the opportunity the law grants to show love to God. God's perfect heart of love seeks to protect the productivity of people. Stealing harms people who have worked hard by taking away the fruits of the labor they rightfully earned. God is loving us by letting us know of this command and the consequences that come with breaking it, but he is also giving us a chance to demonstrate our love for him.

The command against stealing comes to us in a world of limited resources, which is, therefore, a world of great need. All of us know what it is to face a lack of financial resources. We are hit with a massive medical bill, our car breaks down, the mortgage is overdue, we are out of groceries, we owe more in taxes than we anticipated. When these things happen, they confront us with a direct choice in our relationship to God. We can choose to have love for God and trust in his love for us by believing he will provide everything we truly need (2 Corinthians 9:10). Or we can respond hatefully to him by attempting to take from another what God has not given to us.

The act of stealing is an act of hatred against God because it doubts God's loving commitment to provide for us and denies that his commands are loving, right, and best. Stealing is a hateful demonstration of our doubt in God's love to provide for us. Refusing to take what God has not given is an expression of our loving trust in God to give us what we need.

When Jesus says, *if you love me, you will keep my commandments,* he is making clear that obedience, rather than being a burdensome occasion for guilt, is a joyful opportunity to show love to the God who is righteousness, demands righteousness, and desires to have a relationship with people he is making increasingly righteous.

Obedience to God's Law Demonstrates Our Love for Others

One more way that the law of God demonstrates the love of God is by giving God's people an opportunity to share their love with others. One of the main ways we love other people is by obeying the law of God: "By this we know that we love the children of God, when we love God and obey his commandments" (1 John 5:2). John wants people to be characterized by a spirit of love for others. This passage gives the proof that we really love others as we have been called to love them, and that proof is that we love God and obey him. The opposite is also true, that you do not really love people if you do not keep God's commands. God's law does not only tell us how to establish relationship with him but also instructs us how to enter into relationship with others. God's commands tell us how to love others.

The demand to tell the truth shows love to others (Ephesians 4:25). Lying does not just dishonor God, who exemplifies honesty and integrity; it also undermines personal relationships. My own life made this clear to me because I grew up as a liar. Before my mom became a follower of Jesus, she was a dishonest person and trained me and my twin brother to lie from an early age.

My mom was a drunk who used lies to cover up her drinking, and she trained me and my brother to lie to help provide cover stories for her bad behavior. The problem with being trained to lie this way was that, as a sinner myself, I enjoyed it. I saw that lies could get me things the truth could not, and I began to lie all the time about everything. I lied about being rich when we were poor. I lied about trips we took all over the world though I scarcely ever left my own town. I lied about being friends with famous people even though my teachers were the most noteworthy people I knew.

I lied a lot and got a reputation for it. One day I told some ridiculous lie to my friend Matt. He just rolled his eyes, waved his hand, and said he didn't believe me because I always lied.

I knew I had a reputation for dishonesty, and I hated it along with the relational tension it created, but I truly didn't know how to stop. I was a slave to sin and needed help. When I became a Christian my freshman year of high school, the very first sin that God convicted me of was my dishonesty.

I began a process of deep repentance and change, and in the great kindness of God, he transformed me into a man who loves the truth. Today, my family and relationships are all characterized by speaking the truth to one another. My ministry is one of speaking and writing about the truth of God. My relationships now are so much richer than they were when I was a kid, because they are defined by loving expressions of the truth. I would never want to go back to the pain and heartbreak that marked my relationships when I was a liar.

God's law is about God's love. This is true whether the law of God is revealing God's loving character and his love for us, giving us an opportunity to love him, or showing us how to love. Law is a loving expression of the great love of God, and a life of law keeping is a life caught up in the great love of God. He reveals his love through his law and invites us, through our observance of the law, to participate in his love.

CONCERNS ABOUT GOD'S LOVE AND GOD'S LAW

Even when we bring God's law into the orbit of his love, it still creates concerns for some. Some people simply cannot understand how to fit obedience together with a relationship of love. Difficult issues exist at the intersection of love and obedience, so I'll briefly address two of them here.

Legalism

The first concern is legalism. When obedience to God's law comes up, religious-sounding people often make the charge of legalism. You don't need any background with any religion at all to know that whatever legalism is, it is bad. Most people would never want to bear the insult of being called a legalist. The word is full of negative connotations that make people very uncomfortable. Legalism is a very bad thing, but we must be sure we understand what it is.

I'll explain two different kinds of legalism. The first kind of legalism is the belief that sinful human beings can obey God's law on their own and please God through their good behavior. This is not true. The Bible teaches that in our sin we have wandered away from God like lost sheep (Isaiah 53:6), that we do not desire God (Romans 3:10–11), that we cannot obey God's law (Romans 8:7), and that we are hopelessly dead in trespasses and sins (Ephesians 2:1). A legalist in this first sense cannot have a relationship with God because he comes to God on the wrong terms, believing that he can draw near to God based on what he has done through his attempts at good behavior. The Bible teaches instead that we can only draw near to God because of what he has done in his love: "When the goodness and loving kindness of God our Savior appeared, he saved us, not because of works done by us in righteousness, but according to his own mercy" (Titus 3:4–5).

There is another kind of legalist, however. It is possible to draw near to God, to trust his love as the basis of your relationship, and still be guilty of legalism. The second manifestation of legalism arises when God's people make up rules of their own for the purpose of relating to God. They make demands that God himself has not made. Sometimes they do this out of care and concern, desiring to avoid any chance of disobedience. Good intentions notwithstanding, many problems flow from making rules that God has not.

One massive problem is that we sin by making our own additions to the Bible (Deuteronomy 12:32; Revelation 22:18). Another problem is that when we add to God's law, instead of loving people, we make their lives harder with legal burdens they cannot carry. Jesus says that legalists "tie up heavy burdens, hard to bear, and lay them on people's shoulders" (Matthew 23:4). Perhaps the most serious problem with this manifestation of legalism is that it mischaracterizes God. We saw earlier that God's law reflects God's character. When we demand that people follow our rules, we are revealing our character and not God's. Legalism places the legalist in the place of God and makes it harder for people to know the character of the one true God.

Our care in expressing the danger of legalism must not forbid us from expressing another danger as well. Sometimes we confuse a proper resistance to legalism with our sinful opposition to God's law. Obedience is not legalism. Obedience demonstrates love for God. Laws are loving expressions of our relationship with God.

Of course, our relationship with God does not begin with obedient law keeping. Nor can our relationship with God be based on rules we make that God never mentioned. Those are each different manifestations of dangerous legalism. But the Bible is more than clear that rules frame our loving relationship with God after he brings us into a relationship with himself by faith: "We are his workmanship, created in Christ Jesus for good works, which God prepared beforehand, that we should walk in them" (Ephesians 2:10). The Bible promises blessings in your relationship with God when you follow his law: "The one who looks into the perfect law, the law of liberty, and perseveres, being no hearer who forgets but a doer who acts, he will be blessed in his doing" (James 1:25). We must always be wary of legalism but never wary of loving obedience that comes to us as a loving gift of God's grace.

Conditions

Another problem raised in connection with God's love and God's law is the presence of conditional statements in the Bible. Conditional statements promise God's blessing not absolutely but in the event that people follow God's commands. There are hundreds of examples in the Bible of statements like this. One significant example comes after the statement of the second of the Ten Commandments. God has commanded his people not to try and create any image of God and says, "You shall not bow down to them or serve them; for I the LORD your God am a jealous God, visiting the iniquity of the fathers on the children to the third and fourth generation of those who hate me, but showing steadfast love to thousands of those who love me and keep my commandments" (Deuteronomy 5:9–10).

This is a classic example of a conditional statement. Blessings and curses are promised based on people's response of faithfulness to God. Many wonder how the God of great love could attach conditions to his affection. Do statements like this mean there are strings attached to God's love? This important question must be answered in a few ways.

The first response is that any relationship we ever have with God is based on his love. "We love because he first loved us" (1 John 4:19). God gives us every good gift. He reveals himself to us, he sends his Son to die for us, and he opens our hearts to believe the truth and trust in Jesus. Our works never initiate a relationship with God. This was true with God's people in the Old Testament standing at the base of Mount Sinai receiving the Ten Commandments.

God remembered his people languishing in Egypt and sent Moses as a deliverer to rescue his people from the hand of Pharoah. He led them through the desert by a pillar of fire and smoke, and he accomplished their miraculous delivery in their journey through two walls of water in the Red Sea. The Bible makes clear that all these things happened simply because he loved his people:

> You are a people holy to the LORD your God. The LORD your God has chosen you to be a people for his treasured possession, out of all the peoples who are on the face of the earth. It was not because you were more in number than any other people that the LORD set his love on you and chose you, for you were the fewest of all peoples, but it is because the LORD loves you and is keeping the oath that he swore to your fathers, that the LORD has brought you out with a mighty hand and redeemed you from the house of slavery, from the hand of Pharoah king of Egypt. (Deuteronomy 7:6–8)

God's relationship with his people is never initiated by their work but by his love. God lavishes promises, provision, and protection on his people so that they are brought close to him. It was true with his people in the exodus from Egypt, and it is true with you.

Notice the relational language in the statement in Deuteronomy 5. God displayed an intense and jealous desire for an exclusive relationship with his people. It talks about his steadfast love for those who love him and his response to those who hate him. This language of exclusivity, love, and hate is relational language.

God desires a loving connection with his people. After God initiates that relationship with his love, we respond with love of our own. We then long for a deeper relationship with the God whose character is revealed in his law. That love causes people to honor the terms of the relationship with God himself. Disobedience shows that you do not know the God of the Bible, do not want him, and will not follow him. Obedience proves the opposite. *If you love me*, Jesus says, *you will keep my commandments.*

Conditional statements in the Bible do not indicate a "strings attached" love. Far from it. Conditional statements express that God is not interested in dragging people near to him who never have an interest in and love for him. God wants a dynamic relationship of love with his people. Conditional statements give us confidence that we can know we really love God: "By this we may know that we are in him: whoever says he abides in him ought to walk in the same way in which he walked" (1 John 2:5–6).

AN OBEDIENT LIFE OF LOVE

The Bible is full of examples of God's people responding to his love with faithful obedience, but one man who has important lessons for us is Joseph, the husband of Mary, mother of Jesus, one of the most delightful characters in the entire biblical narrative. He doesn't get a lot of press—we don't know a ton about him, and by the time Jesus's childhood is over, we never see him again.

God embraced Joseph in his love and reshaped him. He became a man marked by obedience. Every time Joseph is mentioned in the Bible, he is doing what he was told. Joseph obeyed the government and took his pregnant wife to Judea to be registered (Luke 2:1–5). He obeyed the law of God, presenting Jesus in the temple (Luke 2:22). He obeyed the direct command of God and married his pregnant fiancée and kept her a virgin (Matthew 1:24–25). He obeyed the Word of God and called the name of the heavenly child Jesus (Matthew 1:25). And he obeyed God's word to relocate his family to safety not once (Matthew 2:13–15) but twice (Matthew 2:19–20).

Joseph was always obeying. The consistent portrayal of this singular man every time he is mentioned is his devotion to obey God's Word. And the Bible explains why he obeyed when it describes Joseph simply as a righteous man (Matthew 1:19). One of the most illustrious individuals in all human history was defined by righteous obedience to the Word of God. There are so many lessons to learn from his life of obedience.

God's love reshaped Joseph into a man who was characterized by immediate obedience. You see the immediacy of Joseph's obedience every time he gets instructions from divine angels about what he was to do. When God told him to marry a pregnant virgin, he did it without question (Matthew 1:24). When God told him to move to Egypt to protect the life of Jesus, he packed up and went to Egypt (Matthew 2:14). Then, when God told him to pack up and move back to Israel, he packed up and went back to Israel (Matthew 2:21). Joseph's obedience was not reluctant and halting but immediate and eager. Our obedience must look this way. Of course, delayed obedience is better than not obeying at all (Matthew 21:28–31), but the best kind of obedience is like Joseph's. "I hasten and do not delay to keep your commandments" (Psalm 119:60).

God's love reshaped Joseph into a man who obeyed even when it was hard. This makes the immediacy of Joseph's obedience even more remarkable. It is one thing to obey an easy command. It is another thing to obey a command that is hard.

The commands given to Joseph were hard. He was commanded to marry a virgin and to keep her a virgin until Jesus was born. This is a challenging command in so many ways. As soon as Joseph determined to marry the only woman in history who was pregnant out of wedlock while maintaining her moral purity, the difficulty of his life was dramatically increased. We know that Mary was pregnant from the Holy Spirit. Everyone else would have been wrongly convinced that Mary was pregnant because she was immoral. For Joseph to marry such a woman would have implicated him in the sin and ruined his reputation as a righteous man.

Then, of course, there is the difficulty of the marriage. Not many men in history marry a woman knowing that they must avoid the honeymoon or be guilty of sin. This would have been a disappointment for anyone, and it was a disappointment for Joseph. It reminds us that obedience not only should be embraced when it is hard but it can be.

Finally, God's love reshaped Joseph into a man who received the blessings of obedience. Joseph obeyed hard commands and experienced great blessing for it. When obedience is controversial, it is important to remember that commands are not only the terms of our relationship with a God of infinite holiness but they also describe the path to a successful and flourishing life.

Can you imagine how much less jealousy, murder, brokenness, and disease would exist if everyone was faithful to their spouse in marriage? Can you imagine how much more safe, calm, secure, and wealthy our society would be if no one ever stole anything? Can you imagine the happy thriving childhoods of people living in a world without ridicule or bullying? Obedience is good because it results in a life that is good. And Joseph received wonderful blessings for his obedience.

Think of Mary, a young girl scared to death over the messianic embryo in her body. Even though she was on a divine mission, she would have been ridiculed as a harlot. Joseph, though, obediently stood by her. Only eternity will tell the comfort and love she felt in the stable as he stood by her side making sure everything was alright.

Then there was the blessing that came to Joseph as the earthly father of the Son of God. This assignment would be overwhelming to be sure. In the midst of these challenges, however, Joseph got the unspeakable privilege of snuggling Jesus before bed and being the first to speak the stories of Scripture into his perfect little ears. His obedience ensured his part in God's gift of salvation to humanity. Joseph knew the blessings of obedience better than most. You can know those blessings too. Blessed is the man who delights in the law of the LORD (Psalm 1:1–2).

Perhaps you're reading this and you're encouraged by the example of Joseph. You long to live a life captivated by immediate and faithful obedience even when it is hard. Maybe your heart desires the blessing that comes from that sort of obedience, and you long for it with all your heart. You may even want it all the more because you have witnessed in your own life the bitter fruit of disobedience. The point I want to make now is for those who may be encouraged by the example of Joseph but don't know how the faithfulness that characterized him could ever be true about you.

If the prospect of your own obedience discourages you, it is because you are not thinking properly about how to obey. You're not understanding how any human being who has ever lived, except Jesus, could get the label *righteous*. The apostle Paul reminds you with these crucial words from Galatians 3:11, "Now it is evident that no one is justified before God by the law, for 'The righteous shall live by faith.'" This passage describes the only path to righteousness for all people, whether Joseph or you, and the path is not through righteousness that grows out of our own heart.

At the beginning of this chapter, I explained that controversy over obedience stems from frustration over human efforts to keep the law. Well, Paul addresses that controversy by explaining our inability to keep the law. Paul says that it is evident that you cannot be acceptable to God by your own strenuous efforts to keep the law. Instead, if you are to be righteous, you must have faith in the righteous obedience of Jesus Christ. When you trust Jesus, he will give you his own righteousness so that you can be righteous.

God will embrace you in his love and reshape you into an increasingly obedient person. Even our response of loving obedience to God requires a gift of God's love. That is a gift that comes through Jesus. It is a gift that is received by faith. It is the gift of obedience to anyone who believes.

CHAPTER 12

The Best Day of Your Life

Perfect love casts out fear.

1 JOHN 4:18

At the end of this part of our journey into the heart of God, I want to describe to you—whoever you are—the best day you will ever experience. On the way to describing that very best day, I want to tell you about one of the worst of mine.

To appreciate the grief of that day, you need to know that, for my entire childhood, my dad was the best man I ever knew. I loved him with all my heart even though I was not his biological child. From the moment my mom announced her pregnancy, he knew it was impossible that he could be the father of the twins in her body. And yet that shameful knowledge never impeded his full display of fatherly affection. In a now-faded photograph—the first picture ever taken of me in the hospital when I was born—you see me cradled in one of his strong arms, my twin brother cradled in the other, and the bright smile of my dad beaming between us.

From that day forward, he took us to school, cared for us when we were sick, pushed us on the swings, scolded us when we disobeyed, comforted us when we were sad, walked with us in the park, took us for ice cream at Berryman's, taught us how to fish, flew kites with us in the high school parking lot, told us "secret stories," made homemade French fries in the FryDaddy, let us ride in the back of his pickup truck, and played Kenny Rogers on the record player as loud as we wanted. He also spent a lot of time trying to protect us from our mother, who was always unstable, often drunk, and typically violent. That is where my story edges closer to the dreadful day I mentioned.

My mom's unstable existence—long before she became a Christian later in life—meant it was typically not safe to live with her. She was violently abusive and neglectful, and the constant custody battles between her and my dad had us regularly in court. Those court battles were frustrating. On the one hand, it was obvious to everyone that we had an unfit mother and a responsible father who loved us. On the other hand, though my dad's name was on my birth certificate, there was a paternity test and legal ruling that I was the biological son of another man. That reality combined, at times, with a blind preference that children should be with their mothers meant that in my entire childhood, my dad never possessed more than temporary custody of me. When I was in the fifth grade, Dad got us for two whole years—the longest stretch of our lives.

Those two years were the happiest of my young life. I was terrified of my mother and hated life with her back then, but I loved my dad. He was kind, funny, generous, and safe. During those incredible years, I spent the days Dad worked at Mammaw's house and the evenings with him. At night we watched fishing shows and golf tournaments, we caught crawdads in the creek, and we ate his famous grilled cheeseburgers. Every Friday night, we would watch a movie and eat pepperoni pizza with extra cheese. My dad was the best. But those wonderful days were not to last.

The same legal drama that granted custody to my father took it away from him. After two years cleaning up her life, Mom came out of nowhere to take us back again. She had moved away from our little town in eastern Kentucky to a city far away, and she wanted another chance at being a good mom. Looking back as an adult, I really appreciate what she was trying to do, but my boyish heart couldn't understand it. I was barely able to handle the news that I would be moving away from my father to live with my mother in a massive, distant, scary place.

That terrible day happened on a gray Kentucky afternoon in the dead of winter. My mom showed up with her boyfriend to load my things and move me away from the comfort, warmth, trust, and love of my father's home. I still remember the plunging feeling in my stomach when I looked out the window and saw that red truck approaching like a hearse.

In a display of resistance, I had not packed any of my belongings, so the process of departure took a very long time. In that long stretch of time, every engagement was awkward between a heartbroken boy, a brash boyfriend, a grief-stricken father, and a mom aware of the pain she was inflicting. As awkward as it all was, it could not compare to the final interaction I had with my father before I left my home.

That last moment with my dad was the darkest of my sad childhood. He had carried the last of my possessions to the truck and came back in and stood in the door. A soft, puffy coat protected him from the freezing temperatures outside. He looked at me from the door with grim knowledge that this was the end.

I ran to him, he fell to his knees, and my precious father pulled me into his loving embrace. No devoted dad ever held his son so close. His strong arms drew me in more tightly, and we both heaved guttural sobs. I could smell the cold from his coat, I felt the whiskers from his neck, and I heard his mournful voice as he moaned through tears how much he loved me. Physically unable to say goodbye, and with Mom saying it was time to go, that precious embrace ended, and we parted.

I have never been able to tell that story without tears. Tears are streaming from eyes as I write even now over thirty years later. The reason that day was so terrible and causes such pain decades later is because that embrace with my father could not last. When it ended, I got into a red truck and watched through the back window as my dad got further away. I would see him again, but for the rest of my life I would never live with him. The most loving embraces are sad when they are temporary.

LOVE THAT LASTS

All of us who want to experience love's embrace—to drive away the bitterness in our culture, the loneliness in our lives, and the sorrow in our hearts—are looking for an embrace that lasts. We want a love that doesn't end. We want love that doesn't come and go but comes and stays. We long for a permanent embrace of love. That is the loving embrace that God gives to his people.

One of the greatest things the Bible says about the great love of God is that it never ends: "Oh give thanks to the LORD, for he is

THE BEST DAY OF YOUR LIFE

good, for his steadfast love endures forever!" (Psalms 106:1; 107:1; 118:1, 29; 136:1). God's love never ends, and when you trust in him, your experience of his love never ends. Jesus says the Father has "given him authority over all flesh, to give eternal life to all whom you have given him. And this is eternal life, that they know you, the only true God, and Jesus Christ whom you have sent" (John 17:2–3). Eternal life is the miraculous gift of God where he brings us into his experience of forever to know his love. It is God's delight to join his people to his experience of eternal, boundless, and unmediated love.

The enjoyment of divine love forever is what John means when he says, "Perfect love casts out fear" (1 John 4:18). He is talking about the fear that every person has of their eventual death and ultimate judgment (1 John 4:17). Deep in the heart of every human soul is the awareness that no matter how good we say we are, in truth we are guilty and deserve judgment. In spite of how healthy we eat or how young we try to look, the conviction clings to every person that each day of our life brings us a step closer to the end of it. This reality is called the fear of death (Hebrews 2:15).

John wages war against the fear of death with the great love of God when he says *perfect love casts out fear*. Jesus says, "Whoever hears my word and believes him who sent me has eternal life. He does not come into judgment but has passed from death to life" (John 5:24). This is a guarantee that your experience of the love of God will never end, not even in your death.

One day everything you know and love about this life will come to an end. You may get a diagnosis that gives you time to plan, prepare, and grieve, or death may come quickly and without warning. The end of your precious life may come peacefully or with pain. But your death will come. One day, whether you are aware of it or not, you will see your final sunset, you will take your last breath, taste your final meal, give a final hug to a friend, and say goodbye to a loved one for the last time. On that day, your heart will beat one last time, and you will close your eyes in death.

That day will be your very best day. The glory of that day will not be found in the pain and loss leading up to it but in the joy and love flowing from it. Throughout this book I have talked about the embrace of divine love. I have shared my experience of this embrace and the experience of others from Abraham to the prodigal son. I have shared these stories so that you too could be wrapped in God's embrace of love.

My repeated references to this embrace are a metaphor I use to describe a spiritual reality. God's embrace of you in his love is a *real* embrace but not a physical one. Speaking more literally, this spiritual embrace is really an awareness of God's love that happens when you apply the concrete truth of God's love to your particular situation. When you know, trust, believe, and are convinced of God's love for you, that is when you experience his embrace. And God's embrace of love comes through your faith in that love. In this life, it comes and goes. God's great love for you is perfect and constant, but your awareness of it is sporadic and temporary.

The best day of your life will happen when you are welcomed home to be with Jesus and experience the full, physical, and permanent embrace of God. Death is your last enemy and serves as the entrance into a full and unmediated experience of divine love: "We are of good courage, and we would rather be away from the body and at home with the Lord" (2 Corinthians 5:8). When the apostle Paul writes these words, he is not dreading the day of his death, but looking forward to it as the time to leave our halting experience of the love of God and enter the full expression of it. *Perfect love casts out fear.*

On the glorious day when you see God face to face, you will be transfixed in a resplendent display of infinite, glorious, and great love. You will not have to fight to believe in God's love anymore; you will only delight to receive it. The great God of heaven and Earth will appear in your gaze and wrap you in a miraculous, powerful, and delightful embrace of his love that will never end. He will pull you close in a way that dries up all your sad tears and draws out all your happy ones.

You will exist in his love forever. You will enjoy the life your heart has always longed for with friends and family all surrounded in perfect love. It will be beyond better than anything you could ever imagine. It will be the best day of your life. And best of all, it will be just the beginning of a glorious and eternal embrace in the great love of God that will never end.

Acknowledgments

The existence of 1 John 4:7 in the Bible requires me to acknowledge the massive help I received in writing this book. It says, "Beloved, let us love one another, for love is from God, and whoever loves has been born of God and knows God." One truth that passage teaches is that the beloved people of God show his love through our acts of love. I have seen the great love of God in countless acts of love from numerous people in the writing of this book.

I must first thank the amazing Christians at the First Baptist Church of Jacksonville. My primary ministry is to love them, walk with them, pray for them, and share God's truth with them. They have walked with me and my family, loving us and supporting us, for the last seven years. I have never encountered a better, more faithful body of believers. I love them with all my heart. There is no way this book would exist without their love for me. In particular, I am thankful for the great delight of serving with twenty other pastors who love me, tell me the truth, and graciously read an early draft of this book.

I am also incredibly grateful for two assistants, Amy Evenson and Caroline Haley. They have each worked with me closely for many years. They walked with me during the experiences that led to this book and during the writing of it. They made time in my schedule for research, processing, and writing. They let me bounce ideas off them. They each carefully read several drafts of the manuscript. They are delightful Christian women, it is my honor to serve with them, and I love them.

Renee Hoskins is one of the most wonderful people I have ever met in my life. I first met her on the front row of one of my classes at Southern Seminary. She quickly became one of my very best students and has been close with my family ever since. After years of being a student and employee of mine, she is now married to one of the pastors at my church. She is brilliant, and I don't like writing things that she doesn't review. She faithfully read and commented on several drafts of this manuscript while she was very pregnant with her third child. I love her and am incredibly grateful for all her work on this book.

My relationship with Zondervan began at a lunch meeting with Ryan Pazdur eleven years ago. He has worked with me on every project with them since that lunch. There is a lot I love about working with Zondervan, but my favorite is Ryan. He carefully reads all my work without being afraid to tell me the truth about what is not working and how I could make it better. He is a wise, godly, and delightful co-laborer. He is also my friend. Sometimes I can't tell if I like writing books or if I just like working with Ryan. In any case, this book would not have happened without his diligent labor.

Being a pastor's kid is tough. It often means that, simply because of who your dad is, people unfairly scrutinize your life. As hard as it is, I can't imagine that there are any three children who have ever done it better than my two wonderful sons, Carson and Connor, and my delightful daughter, Chloe. One of the greatest honors of my life is to live with them, laugh with them, and be laughed at by them. They have contributed immeasurably to the writing of this book. On the days of my life when I have been most cruelly mistreated, I have always come home to them and seen a living demonstration of the love of God. Each one of them made it into the pages of this book, and we have a rule in our house that I never tell stories about them without their permission. So I am thankful that they allowed me to share some of their story with you.

The greatest helper to me under heaven is my wife, Lauren. This book had its origin in the most painful ministry ordeal either of us have ever experienced. Each of us would say it was the hardest, most painful, most extreme situation we have ever endured. Throughout the hardest years of this ordeal, Lauren never wavered. She told me the truth when I was disoriented, she encouraged me when I was down, she cared for me physically when I could not feed myself or even use the bathroom. I sometimes wonder how she could love me so much. I never wonder that she loves me with all her heart. I love her right back and am more thankful for her than any gift from God I have ever received.

The Bible is clear that every good gift and every perfect gift comes from God (James 1:17). That means the good gift of this book and all the people who surrounded me as I wrote it ultimately come from the God of great love. I look back at the hardest season of my life and am thankful for it because in that difficulty I was able to meet him in a powerful way I never had before. The hard years leading up to this book were made wonderful by the delightful embrace of God's love that I experienced. Through Jesus, he has saved me, changed me, upheld me, and restored me. He is the very best friend I have ever had or could ever have. I find it impossible to convey in words how grateful I am for the privilege of knowing him, being loved by him, and telling others about him.

Heath Lambert
Jacksonville, Florida
June 2022